5 February 2008 - aetatis meae xxxix - Chicago - Powell's -

TWENTY QUESTIONS

TWENTY QUESTIONS

(POSED BY POEMS)

1. _____?

2. _____?

3. _____?

4. _____?

5. _____?

6. _____?

7. _____?

8. _____?

9. _____?

10._____?

J . D . McCLATCHY

COLUMBIA UNIVERSITY PRESS
New York

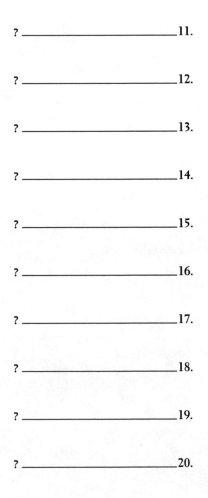

COLUMBIA UNIVERSITY PRESS
New York   Chichester, West Sussex
Publishers Since 1873
Copyright © 1998
Columbia University Press
All rights reserved

Library of Congress
Cataloging-in-Publication Data
McClatchy, J. D.
Twenty questions / J. D. McClatchy.
p.   cm.
ISBN 0-231-11172-X
1. McClatchy, J. D., 1945-
—Authorship.
2. Poetry.   I. Title.
PS3563.A26123T9   1998
811'.54—dc21   97-49622
                                CIP

Casebound editions of
Columbia University Press books are
printed on permanent and durable acid-
free paper.

Printed in the United States of America
Designed by Chip Kidd
c 10 9 8 7 6 5 4 3 2 1

For Chip Kidd

CONTENTS

ACKNOWLEDGMENTS

Some of the chapters in this book appeared elsewhere. Most have been revised, and several retitled. They were first published as follows:

"Reading," in Michael Dorris and Emilie Buchwald, eds., *The Most Wonderful Books* (Minneapolis: Milkweed Editions, 1997).

"My Fountain Pen," in Patrick Merla, ed., *Boys Like Us* (New York: Avon, 1996).

"Commonplaces," in Stephen Kuusisto, Deborah Tall, and David Weiss, eds., *The Poet's Notebook* (New York: Norton, 1995).

"Twenty Questions," in the *Princeton University Library Chronicle* 55, 3 (Spring 1994).

"Reading Pope," in Robert Pack and Jay Parini, eds., *Touchstones* (Middlebury: Middlebury College Press, 1995).

"Aspects of 'Battle-Piece,' " in *Salmagundi* 87 (Summer 1990).

"Woman in White," in J. D. McClatchy, ed., *Woman in White: Selected Poems of Emily Dickinson* (London: Folio Society, 1991).

"Wildness Asking for Ceremony," in Jean Garrigue, *Selected Poems* (Urbana: University of Illinois Press, 1992).

"At Her Other Desk," in the *New York Times Book Review*, April 17, 1994.

"Laughter in the Soul," in *Antaeus* 71/72 (Autumn 1993).

"Songs of a Curmudgeon," in the *New York Times Book Review*, May 21, 1989.

"The Exile's Song," in the *New Republic*, December 1, 1987.

"Chiselled Breath," in *Partisan Review*, 57, 1 (1990).

"Sitting Here Strangely on Top of the Sunlight," in the *New York Times Book Review*, June 17, 1990.

"The Lost Upland," in the *New Yorker*, June 3, 1996.

"Encountering the Sublime," in *Verse* 5, 2 (July 1988).

"Braving the Elements," in the *New Yorker*, March 27, 1995.

"Masters," in *Pequod* 28/29 (1989).

"Battle-Piece" is reprinted by kind permission of Ben Belitt from *Possessions: New and Selected Poems (1938–1985)* (Boston: Godine, 1986).

TWENTY QUESTIONS

A WORD FIRST

If, as Oscar Wilde claimed, all criticism is autobiography, let me preface this book with two more memories. When I was growing up, after the war, the suburbs were not quite complete. The one I was raised in, on the fringe of Philadelphia, still had a couple of odd properties, and they became the poles of my imagination. One, near the public high school, was a small working farm, always referred to as Toland's Farm. I can easily recall the wonder of walking down three blocks of neat stone and stucco family houses, then wedging backward through a tall hedge and finding myself in a billowing pasture. I loved spending time at Toland's Farm: the smell of meadow grass and cow dung, the iridescent feathers on the rooster, the green slime of hen droppings, their warm eggs in the straw, the horse's slobber, the cobblestone barnyard. And if I set out from home in the opposite direction, toward the railroad station, there was Gibson's Woods. This was—or seemed—an immense walled-in forest, complete with grotto, brookside stone hut, paths, and log roads, all surrounding a castle that some local banker's wife thought she had once seen in France and asked to have duplicated. If it was not a castle exactly, at least there were granite walls, high windows through which I could spy a tapestried, chandeliered ballroom, and a tower with its slate witch's-cap spire. When, years later, I read Alain-Fournier, I realized what it all represented: a sort of magical demesne. I would play in this three-dimensional fairy tale by the hour, imagining myself wizard or wanderer. And these, then, were what first drew out my imagination: nature and fantasy, the domestic life turned inside out.

The appeal that poems make to me has always seemed similarly doubled. As a child, I never read poetry and disdained novels. My favorite reading was, oh, *The Lives of the Saints* or *The Lives of the Noble Greeks and Romans*, Paul de Kruif's *Microbe Hunters* or Clarence Darrow's autobiography. The elegant and compelling arrangement of facts seemed to me from the start more exciting than the easy self-indulgence of make-believe. It was not until, in high school, I was scared by a poem that I began properly to value fantasy. The poem assigned that day was Wallace Stevens's "The Emperor of Ice Cream." I didn't understand a word of it. My annoyance soon gave way—as the poem floated mockingly further off—to real anxiety. And when, a few days later, still not understanding the poem but starting to enjoy its morbid flippancies, I was able to convert my fear into a pleasure, I found myself ironically closer to the origins and spirit of the poem itself.

A sensibility is formed to read as well as to write. There are *styles* of reading. And like the poem itself, an essay about the poem is a distillation of watery thoughts, a concentration of impulses. Once asked about his critical method, T. S. Eliot replied, "The only method is to be very intelligent." In part, he meant a criticism pitched at the level of the poem; he meant a reading whose tact and respect, whose ambition and canniness are a match for the poem's own intentions and textures. It's always seemed to me that poets are best suited to this sort of reading; that their own styles, instinct with metaphor, are an answering echo to the original poem's voice. Someone once characterized the short story as "a wish modified by a truth." But what he was, in effect, defining was the whole process of *reading*: the way we read fictions, and the way our fictions "read" experience. A poet's *wishes*—the impulses and obsessions of his or her imagination—are urged into rhythms and lines, subjects and stanzas, shaped to point toward some emerging or retreating emotional and moral *truth*. The best critics—by which I mean the most useful—often start with truths, and work backward toward the wish. They reveal the sorrow at the heart of affirmation, the pleasure in the arguments of melancholy. They want to complicate our responses to a text by unsettling our convictions. They want to restore to a poem the life it has given them: a shape to their feelings, a weight to their ambitions, an edge to their thoughts. They acknowledge the claims of both the poem's wishes and its truth. They ask questions.

This is a book of questions, not answers. It begins with several autobiographical chapters about how certain questions occurred to me, but that is as much as to say they are less about myself than about A Reader. Reading is musing. *Musing* is a term that catches up the notion of spellbound inspiration: drifting slowly in a punt down the river of a text, one hand over the side, fingers dipped into the eddying implications. But in fact the word is thought to derive from the Medieval Latin *musum*, or snout. What readers do is *nose around* in a text, like moles or pigs, sniffing and tunneling, following a trail of evidence through the literature of the past, or rooting for dream-truffles.

There follows a group of essays about individual poets and poems, and the questions they raise. I have wanted to look at the work of neglected poets like Jean Garrigue and Ben Belitt, and lavish on what's been forgotten all that I can remember of a life and how it has been refigured in poems. With more familiar poets—James Wright, W. S. Merwin, Philip Larkin, Seamus Heaney, Richard Wilbur, or James Merrill—I have tried to lay out the terms of a career, the topography of an imagination, and not just the behavior of a specific book. Or I have looked at an imagination—Elizabeth Bishop's, say, or Stephen Sondheim's—from an unusual angle, hoping thereby to observe sides of the literary mind that are turned away from criticism's business-as-usual. When writing about contemporary poets, it is crucial to describe the long family history of their art, the genealogy of masters. In an analogous way, I have also included here two essays about great poets of the past, Alexander Pope and Emily Dickinson, both of whom seem to me astonishingly contemporary in their power. Finally, there is a pair of essays about two classicizing artists, Degas and Horace, whose work is refined, idiomatic, and firsthand, and whose analyses of society are quick-witted and biting, but whose instincts were shaped by a passion for the past.

"Art," said Goethe, "is simply memory organized." How art works with memory, and on it, is the theme of this book. Memory is traditionally the mother of the Muses, the origin of all the arts. But don't memories abide because they are problems? They are the questions we keep for the past, those bits of self that make too much sense or not enough. Individuals remember, art memorializes. To the extent unconscious associations or conscious craft shape our account of experience, we build into the story a certain resistance to the starkness of its truth. Poems are plea bargains. Their maneuvers on trial—their waverings and weavings—are the pathos and exhilaration of the art. But there is more. The way Whitman's poems memorize America, or the way Plath's memorize her father—this too is the work of poetry: to absorb and transfigure the reach of the eye or the underworld of the heart. Poems are private and social acts. That is to say, they withhold themselves from any easy understanding, but make their case out of lives lived in the world, shared histories, implicit common assumptions. This is one reason why, in the essays that follow, I have brought the idiosyncrasies of biography, even of autobiography, to bear on poems. The "personal" does not lie behind but upon a work of art: not Turner lashed to the mast in order to *experience* the storm at sea he will translate into a chaos of colors, but his fingerprint still visible today in the glob of pigment applied to make the sun that drove that storm aside. The baffled self, clutching obsessively at memories, describing and formulating the threats against it, still cannot resist the luxuries of portrayal or the pleasures of performance. Like memories, the voice of a poem and its encrusted surfaces both resist and reveal. Memorable language is meant to help us remember. Remember what? Here is Auden's answer: "Birth, death, the Beatific Vision, the abysses of hatred and fear, the awards and miseries of desire, the unjust walking the earth and the just scratching miserably for food like hens, triumphs, earthquakes, deserts of boredom and featureless anxiety, the Golden Age promised or irrevocably past, the gratifications and terrors of childhood, the impact of nature on the adolescent, the despairs and wisdom of the mature, the sacrificial victim, the descent into Hell, the devouring and benign mother. Yes, all of these, but not these only. Everything that we can remember, no matter how trivial: the mark on the wall, the joke at lunch, word games, these, like the dance of a stoat or the raven's gambol, are equally the subject of poetry." In short, the tale of the tribe and the cry of the single occasion. But there is a price for such remembering. The tension between these two impulses— to reveal and to resist—inflects whatever is said into a question. Memories, like poems, are not what is left to us but what prompt us, not answers but questions. Here, then, are twenty of mine.

1 . READING

?

Because I was the eldest child in my family, and because my father was off fighting in the Pacific, my mother kept an elaborate Baby Book, recording my earliest this and latest that. A few years ago, in a forgotten attic box, she discovered the book and sent it to me. I notice that when I reached age three, she was asked to list my Favorite Outdoor Activities. She's put a line through "Outdoor" (from the start, I was all for the inner, or at least the indoor life), and written: "Books. Records. Puzzles." They are still my favorites.

One puzzle to record here, a half-century later, is my abiding interest in books. I was read to, but my family was not literary. The gilded bindings of their sets of Dickens and Twain gleamed on high shelves. *Time* and *Life* are what I remember on their laps. What am I saying? I was there too! To this day, I like most to read in bed, and I suspect that's because it recalls snuggling into my father's lap, propped on his arm, warm, the book close to my nose, the sound of a man's voice telling me a story I already knew by heart.

But it's not myself I want to talk about. It's books. It's the difference between "reading" and *reading*. I offer three memories, three morals. And a motto.

First, the motto. It's from Goethe: "All great excellence in life or art, at its first recognition, brings with it a certain pain arising from the strongly felt inferiority of the spectator; only at a later period, when we take it into our own culture, and appropriate as much of it as our capacities allow, do we learn to love and esteem it. Mediocrity, on the other hand, may often give us unqualified pleasure; it does not disturb our self-satisfaction, but encourages us with the thought that we are as good as another . . . . Properly speaking, we learn only from those books we cannot judge."

It was not until prep school that I discovered how to read *properly*, and I owe the discovery to a madman. At fourteen I started in on the classics. The Jesuits who ran the school are renowned as taskmasters, and that first year we were drilled in declensions and conjugations. By the following year we were considered ready for Homer, and handed over to the old priest who was to be our guide through the *Odyssey*. As it turned out, several years later he was retired to a mental hospital, but I remain indebted to what were then called merely his "eccentricities." Each night's homework consisted of a long episode to be read, parsed, translated, and *understood*. And our teacher did not think we could truly understand Homer, or his hero's trials, unless we duplicated the circumstances of the poem. To that end, we were told to go each night to the basement of our homes, with a lighted candle and a bowl of applesauce (for its Hellenic tang) — and, between gulped spoonfuls, declaim the Greek, pretending we were in the dank, dark hold of a storm-tossed ship. I was never, before or since, so enthralled to a text. I now realize that what excited me then was not just the story or the theatrics. It was the words themselves. Because the Greek words were strange, I had to *think* about them, about their sound and etymology, their meanings and overtones, how they were combined into sentences and metaphors. The mad old priest was right: *reading* Homer finally involved the same struggle and search, adventures and homecoming Odysseus himself was driven to.

After my sophomore year at Georgetown, I stayed on in Washington for the summer and enrolled, by special permission, in a graduate seminar on Elizabethan literature. Our textbook was the old Hebel and Hudson *Tudor Poetry and Prose*, a massive, closely printed compendium as stuffy as our professor, with his wedge of white hair, steel-rimmed spectacles, and stack of file cards that, having drily relayed the fact or "idea" on each, he would snap like playing cards to the back of the pile. I was intimidated, not by being over my

academic head or by the lackluster recital (actually, for reasons I can now neither recall nor imagine, he inspired me to love Hooker's *Of the Laws of
Ecclesiastical Polity*) but by the enormity and grandeur of the subject. I made
of my apartment that summer a context for my study: curling Hilliard and
Holbein prints on the wall, Julian Bream plucking Dowland on the stereo set.
Still, I was playing at it, accumulating rather than concentrating. Then one
day the assignment was Marlowe's "Hero and Leander" . . .

> On Hellespont, guilty of true love's blood,
> In view, and opposite, two cities stood,
> Sea-borderers, disjoined by Neptune's might;
> The one Abydos, the other Sestos hight.

So the poems begins, and goes on to trace the heavenly path that runs along
Leander's back and the pearl-strewn seabed where, stripped to the ivory skin,
his body comes to rest. I was literally overwhelmed. It rarely matters who precisely initiates you—the old whore in a walkup, a teenager in the locker room,
the telephone lineman picked up at a bar. The experience is decisive. So was
this one. It was the first time I had felt the erotic power of a poem. In retrospect, that seems a crucial moment in anyone's reading life: to fall in love with
a text, to feel its sexual heat, to sense it unbuttoning your shirt.

Some years later I was in graduate school at Yale, a class on American poetry
with Harold Bloom. We were reading Emily Dickinson. At last I was under the
spell of a great teacher, and what he taught me was this: the highest form of
reading is asking hard questions of the text, as one should of a teacher. Bloom
had—probably still has—a classroom manner that is deliberately provocative,
at once gripping and infuriating. Like all great teachers, he merely brooded
aloud. His questions of a poem—"What exactly, my dears, does Miss Dickinson
mean by 'circumference'?"—were nearly always unanswerable, but prompted
endless discussion (abruptly cut off by another oracular question on a different
matter). The effect of these lessons was only felt hours later, at home, in bed
with the book. It was then that I *read* Dickinson, and listened—because I had
been taught to challenge her—as she took the traditional language of belief,
emptied it of any reassurance, then charged it anew with a startling force. In
their own way, her methods mirrored my teacher's . . . and became my teacher.
Reading, I'd been taught, means questioning, sensing that what you read is
unfinished until completed in the self. The first text is the soul. And the last.

2 . Dreaming

?

?

In his *Life of Shelley*, Jefferson Hogg relates a story he once heard about Wordsworth. The poet used to keep pencil and paper by his bedside, and when a thought occurred to him in the night, or he awakened suddenly from a dream, he would write it down instantly, without lighting a candle. Through long habit he was able to write in the dark. When Shelley heard about it, he experimented with this method of retrieving the fading embers of the unconscious. But, it is reported, he usually dropped his pencil, or his paper, and when he managed to hold onto both, in the morning he found the writing was illegible.

I rarely remember my dreams, but when I do they seem to have involved a pretty straightforward—that is, easily decoded—processing of the previous day's agenda of thwarted desires and overdrawn anxieties. There are a few recurring dreams, however. Invariably they are a puzzle to be solved: a vaguely familiar situation into which I am put or have wandered, and which I must escape or master. Just last night, for instance, there was a variant of the most common. I am back in college. It is toward the end of a semester, and I suddenly realize that I haven't been attending an English course I'd signed up for. (It's as likely to be a course in physics or Urdu, but last night it was English.) Exams are approaching and I hadn't any idea what I should have been studying—though I've skipped classes, in part, because I am haughtily convinced I know it all. I find the room and take my seat—last night, I was sitting by chance next to George Plimpton. The teacher is an attractive young black woman. She's explaining a point of grammar, and to illustrate it has positioned several pieces of toast on a shelf attached to the blackboard. Oh, but her point is so obvious, and the others in class seem confused. It has to do with the use of the word *rather* in a sentence. It's clear to me, as to no one else, that the third slice of toast is out of place. . . . Well, this is all too tiresome. My eventual shame and further confusion in that classroom I shall leave to your imagination. The toast reminds me, though, of another matter. Almost the first thing I do every morning after getting up is the *New York Times* crossword puzzle—in pen and rather quickly. I do it as obsessively as I dream certain dreams. It's not the difficulty of the crossword that attracts me, but the reassurance that *here*, in *this* puzzle, for every question there is an answer and for every answer there is a question.

If we move these two terms to the realm of poetry, is a poem more like a *dream* or a *puzzle*? When a reader first encounters a strong poem, it is likely to strike him as a dream—a text replete with meaning that is mysteriously both proffered and withdrawn. Correspondingly, when the idea—or, better to say, instinct—for that poem first glimmered in the poet's own mind, and as he begins to work it up on paper, the poem is also likely to resemble an unfolding dream. Only later, when the poet is revising a final draft, or the reader has understood its depths and implications, will the poem seem to each a puzzle, intricately constructed and apparently solved. But truly great poems—think of a psalm by Emily Dickinson or an ode by Elizabeth Bishop—are puzzles that remain dreams. Let this memory of mine give an example. I was in school, toward the end of the semester. This time—awake and never missing a class— I was in graduate school. My teacher was Cleanth Brooks, one of the most learned and subtle readers of poems, and a man whose method had taught several generations of readers how to approach a poem. He and I were walking down the street one afternoon in New Haven, discussing Wordsworth. "You know," he said, "the older I get, and the more I read Wordsworth, the less

I understand him." He was not, of course, underestimating either's powers; rather, he was acknowledging a fact about all great poets—that the terms of their poetic selfhood, the sublime leaps their poems make, will forsake us if we presume to think we have comprehended them.

With the years, it gets so that what I remember is having had an experience, but I can no longer exactly recall the experience itself. There is a snapshot, not a movie. For instance, I remember that, about thirty years ago, I had a series of vivid dreams about Ben Jonson. He looked rather like the familiar contemporary portrait of him now in the National Portrait Gallery in London: both studious and swaggering, bully and bard. I remember that in my dream he was dressed more raffishly than in his portrait, that we were in a pub, that I was shy and content to listen as he held forth on all manner of topics. But what he said—pretty clear three decades ago, and interesting enough for me to resume the sessions several nights in a row—is lost to me now.

But the other time I dreamt about a writer remains both clear and haunting. I got to know Anne Sexton around 1972. We grew to be friends, and were an odd pair. She was by then a celebrity, and a wreck. But a glamorous and compelling one—constantly looped on vodka and pills, desperately divorced, mentally unstable, dressed to go out on the town in a long red satin dress with her husky voice and raucous laugh. I, on the other hand, was a serious-minded graduate student, nervously gay, wide-eyed. When I first visited her, to do an interview, I arrived at her suburban house on the dot of eleven, as agreed. One of her daughters answered the door, explained that her mother wasn't feeling well and was still in bed, and would I wait in the living room please. An hour passed. The daughter reappeared and asked if I'd follow her upstairs. Mother was still in bed, but would see me there. I was shown into the bedroom. Anne was in the midst of a huge bed, propped up on pillows, in a swank sateen bathrobe. She motioned me to a chair. I mumbled something about not wanting to trouble her. That launched her on an account of her recent woes and illnesses. She wound up with the latest complaint, rubbing her hands over her robe. "And I have very sensitive nipples," she said. "You'll see."

Yikes. I'd only just been introduced. Oh, but all that sorted itself out soon enough, and we became pals. Within a couple of years, she asked if I would serve as her literary executor (I declined)—a request, I only realized later, that was part of a determined and gradual withdrawal that culminated in her suicide. A couple of weeks before she killed herself, she was calling me from the pay phone in a mental hospital, insisting she was receiving radio transmissions in her cavities and would I come check her out of this hellhole. My sympathy pulsed, but even then I knew enough not to intervene. She eventually came home. I called in. And when, one day that I telephoned, I was told by a house-keeper that Anne was in Baltimore, giving a poetry reading, and would return tomorrow, I left word that I'd call back the day after. In fact, I forgot to do so. That night, I had a dream. I was watching the evening news. Walter Cronkite was announcing that the Pulitzer Prize–winning poet Anne Sexton had died, and behind him was an inset showing some sort of grainy home movie of her. She was sitting on a sofa, with a child in her lap. She had on a dress and a hairdo that resembled photographs of my mother when I was small. And the child on her lap, I then noticed, was a young boy, in shorts and a horizontally striped T-shirt, with a buzz cut. I recognized him as well. Sexton had no son. The boy was myself. Early the next morning, the dream throbbed—when, suddenly, the phone rang. It was Howard Moss. He wondered if I'd heard the news. Yesterday, Anne Sexton had committed suicide.

My dream, of course, had to do with my guilt at not having telephoned her when I'd promised to. But the coincidence was more than spooky, and remains as my only (unreal) experience of precognition. I could as easily—as I do now—have read her last poems to see the same unwinding, the same cries and whispers, the same stark refusals. As a reader, instead of as a dreamer, I could have been a child on her lap.

It is no wonder we pay people to listen to our dreams. As an apt analogy, Leopardi suggested would-be poets should underwrite an audience for their poems: hired listeners in a small amphitheater, the size of a steam room, paid to listen, murmur, applaud.

Novalis: "Is sleep a mating with oneself?" Dreams and poems resemble each other in nothing so much as in their autoeroticism.

Nothing, after all, is so logical as a dream. All the connections are there, but dis-guised or concealed. This is why it is not surrealist gibberish that is most dream-like. Nor even those exquisite epiphanic poems by James Wright that are the best of the "deep image" wing. Oh, there are extraordinary waking dreams that mull over the collective unconscious, like James Merrill's *The Changing Light at Sandover*. But, for my money, the most dreamlike poem I know, because it elaborates a private knowledge into a grand myth, is John Hollander's *Reflections on Espionage*. The whole relationship between a master spy and his control is an uncanny trope on the business of dreamwork.

But there is a way too that many strong poems resemble dreams—or perhaps I should say sleep. If we consider the four stages of sleep, each with its distinctive characteristics—light sleep, followed by "spindles" and rolling of eyes, followed by deep sleep with its slower brain waves and lowered heart rate, followed by the deepest sleep of all, out of which the sleeper emerges into the REM state—could we follow a similar pattern in certain poems? We are familiar enough now with the dynamics of REM, that "internal storm" of nearly hallucinatory sensations on which both our psyches and our bodies depend. And now, when I read "Tintern Abbey" or "Ode to a Nightingale" or "The Auroras of Autumn," *The Bridge* or *The Waste Land*, what I sense is this same movement inward, a deeper concentration, then a release of fearsome energies.

Three Dreams About Elizabeth Bishop

I.
It turned out the funeral had been delayed a year.
The casket now stood in the State Capitol rotunda,
An open casket. You lay there like Lenin
Under glass, powdered, in powder blue
But crestfallen, if that's the word
For those sagging muscles that make the dead
Look grumpy. The room smelled of gardenias.
Or no, I *was* a gardenia, part of a wreath
Sent by the Radcliffe Institute and right behind
You, with a view down the line of mourners.
When Lloyd and Frank arrived, both of them
Weeping and reciting—was it "Thanatopsis"?—
A line from Frank about being the brother
To a sluggish clod was enough to wake you up.
One eye, then the other, slowly opened.

You didn't say anything, didn't have to.
You just blinked, or I did, and in another room
A group of us sat around your coffin chatting.
Once in a while you would add a comment—
That, no, hay was stacked with beaverslides,
And, yes, it was a blue, a mimeograph blue
Powder the Indians used, and stuck cedar pegs
Through their breasts in the ghost dance—
All this very slowly. Such an effort for you
To speak, as if underwater and each bubble-
Syllable had to be exhaled, leisurely
Floated up to the surface of our patience.
Still alive, days later, still laid out
In a party dress prinked with sun sparks,
Hands folded demurely across your stomach,
You lay on the back lawn, uncoffined,
Surrounded by beds of freckled foxglove
And fool-the-eye lilies that only last a day.
By then Lowell had arrived, young again
But shaggy even in his seersucker and tie.
He lay down alongside you to talk.
The pleasure of it showed in your eyes,
Widening, then fluttering with the gossip,
Though, of course, you still didn't move at all,
Just your lips, and Lowell would lean in
To listen, his ear right next to your mouth,
Then look up smiling and roll over to tell me
What you said, that since you'd passed over
You'd heard why women live longer than men—
Because they wear big diamond rings.

II.
She is sitting three pews ahead of me
At the Methodist Church on Wilshire Boulevard.
I can make out one maple leaf earring
Through the upswept fog bank of her hair

—Suddenly snapped back, to stay awake.
A minister is lamenting the forgetfulness
Of the laws, and warms to his fable
About the wild oryx "which the Egyptians
Say stands full against the Dog Star
When it rises, looks wistfully upon it,
And testifies after a sort by sneezing,
A kind of worship but a miserable knowledge."
He is wearing, now I look, the other earring,
Which catches a bluish light from the window
Behind him, palm trees bent in stained glass
Over a manger scene. The Joseph sports
A three-piece suit, fedora in hand.
Mary, in a leather jacket, is kneeling.
The gnarled lead joinder soldered behind
Gives her a bun, protruding from which
Two shafts of a halo look like chopsticks.
Intent on her task, her mouth full of pins,
She seems to be taking them out, one by one,
To fasten or fit with stars the night sky
Over the child's crib, which itself resembles
A Studebaker my parents owned after the war,
The model called an Oryx which once took
The three of us on the flight into California.
I remember, leaving town one Sunday morning,
We passed a dwarfish, gray-haired woman
Sitting crosslegged on an iron porch chair
In red slacks and a white sleeveless blouse,
A cigarette in her hand but in a silver holder,
Watching us leave, angel or executioner,
Not caring which, pursuing her own thoughts.

III.
Dawn through a slider to the redwood deck.
Two mugs on the rail with a trace
Still of last night's vodka and bitters.

The windchimes' echo of whatever
Can't be seen. The bottlebrush
Has given up its hundred ghosts,
Each blossom a pinhead firmament,
Galaxies held in place by bristles
That sweep up the pollinated light
In their path along the season.
A scrub jay's Big Bang, the swarming
Dharma of gnats, nothing disturbs
The fixed orders but a reluctant question:
Is the world half-empty or half-full?
Through the leaves, traffic patterns
Bring the interstate to a light
Whose gears a semi seems to shift
With three knife-blade thrusts, angry
To overtake what moves on ahead.
This tree's broken under the day.
The red drips from stem to stem.
That wasn't the question. It was,
Why did we forget to talk about love?
We had all the time in the world.

What we forgot, I heard a voice
Behind me say, was everything else.
Love will leave us alone if we let it.
Besides, the world has no time for us,
The tree no questions of the flower,
One more day no help for all this night.

I wrote "Three Dreams About Elizabeth Bishop" after having indeed
dreamed about her. But only the first section of the poem depends on that
dream. The dream itself was, as I recall, pretty close to what I describe. What
one adds is connective tissue: details that will link together theme and motif,
or set up expectations to be fulfilled later on in the poem. So, in this first section, details like "Thanatopsis," beaverslides, the ghost dance, the foxglove,
even the big-diamond-rings crack . . . these details were added to give texture

or closure to the odd experience of the dream itself. In the end, when they are remembered at all, dreams seem vivid but sketchy, and a poem needs to be subtle and complex as well.

Two days after I started writing up this dream—I was living temporarily in Los Angeles at the time—I happened to go to a concert with my late friend Paul Monette. It was in a church. Sitting there, the idea for the second part of the poem occurred to me. Our ideas, says Wordsworth, are made of old feelings. The dead Bishop—did her very name prompt the thought of her as I sat in my pew?—is resurrected in this second section as a guardian angel. Two photographs crossed in my mind's eye. In a scrapbook, I have a shot of myself, aged four or five, in shorts, an Eton collar and a cap, standing in front of the family Studebaker. The other photograph sits always beside my desk. Rollie McKenna gave it to me: her shot of Elizabeth in an iron chair, taken in Brazil.

The third section of the poem didn't come for the longest time, though the mention of bottlebrush and the scrub jay tells me I must still have been in California when I wrote it. I had the notion that Elizabeth should slowly withdraw from the poem. So, where in the first section she is prominent, in the second part she makes only a cameo appearance. Now, in the finale, she is a disembodied voice. Perhaps that is because here at the end I let my own feelings into the poem, projecting them onto the ghostly figure of the poet. But what I consciously wanted to do here was drive toward the darker side of Bishop's sensibility. The first section highlights the fey, ironic, quizzical, metaphysical side of her imagination. As the poem goes on, I tried to reveal the other side of that bright coin. There is a bitter loneliness to it that I share. Poems about death are poems about love. Poems about love are poems about the imagination. Poems about dreams are poems about death.

3 . MY FOUNTAIN PEN

?

?

?

I hesitate before starting with this particular detail. I want to begin with what for me was a simple fact but what to others may seem a tiresome metaphor. The psychiatrists didn't invent this metaphor, but I suppose they helped popularize and thereby trivialize it. Psychiatrists have never done me any good, so I'll hold my present hesitation against them as well. As I said, for me it was simply a fact: at about the same time I discovered my penis, I started writing with a fountain pen. It was the most sensual thing I had ever held or used. Just to touch it excited me. It was an Esterbrook.

The casing was of a ravenswing purple, with flattop ends and a budded clip. On the side was the silvered lever my fingernail would catch behind and slowly pull to draw the ink upward. I loved dipping it into the little glass mezzanine of ink inside the Scrip bottle, listening to the faint guttural sucking and then gently wiping off the sad excess with a tissue. Why did the whole ritual make the ink seem like blood—blue blood, at least? I would sometimes imagine the squattish ink bottle to be a disgraced but noble Roman senator in his tub. And the nib! Once filled, the capillaries of its ribbed, bee's-body under-

belly ached beneath the pewtery fleur-de-lis. The airhole was a moist miniature of the ink bottle itself, the pen's own private well, in love with the long slit
at the nib's bulbed tip. Down that slit, out from that tip poured the permanent
black-and-blue of my early lessons.

I didn't admire this pen as much as my mother's Sheaffer, and I used often
to take hers from her desk to rub my hand over it. Along with her schoolgirl
toothmarks, there was the white mole and tooled clip on its cap, and a gold
band around its lacquered barrel, itself an iridescent length of striations all
black and eel-grass green, like the shadowy reeds among which a baby in a bas-
ket might be found. The nib was two tiers of fogged copper and iridium, the
airhole was a tiny heart, and the point was sharper. My Esterbrook was what
you would call a starter pen: blunt, cheap, dispensable. It cracked. It spattered.
It leaked. It left an archipelago of small blots on my thumb and middle finger:
the faraway islands of desire. If there was little to admire about it, there was
everything to love.

Long before I was given that fountain pen, of course, I had learned to hide
things. Childhood's true polymorphous perversity, its constant source of both
pleasure and power, is lying. But that pen helped me discover something better than the lie. Almost as soon as it was given to me, I learned to hide inside
the pen. Or rather, the pen allowed me to learn the difference between *hiding*
something and *disguising* something — that is to say, making it difficult but not
impossible to see. Even when I knew the difference, I couldn't always keep
myself from confusing them.

Once for instance — this would have been about 1956, and I was eleven —
I was hopelessly in love with my counselor at summer camp. His name was
Red. It was Red I saw first each morning, shaking me awake, and Red's
drawled fireside stories to which I fell asleep each night. But it was naptime I
liked best: through the eye I pretended was shut I gazed — like some chubby,
crewcut, pimpled Psyche — on Red sleeping: his stubble, his sweatband, the
nipple pressing through his T-shirt, the dream-drool on his chin. On a shelf
over his bunk he had taped up a snapshot of his girlfriend, who stared down
at him with a vacant smile that had none of my cunning, my ardor. When I
asked for his address at summer's end, I gave him a shot of myself. I didn't suppose he'd replace hers with mine, but perhaps I too hoped to keep an eye on
him, from inside a footlocker, say, or from between the pages of a psychology
textbook.

He was on his way that August to enroll as a freshman at the University of Virginia. I returned to my parents' house at the Jersey shore for the last few weeks before more grade school. I spent the time with my old friend the fountain pen, writing letters to Red that transfigured the dull gossip about the camp cook or the impetigo scare at the beach into what I felt were witty, knowing parables of my own superiority and devotion. I never mentioned my family, that I even had a family, or anyone I wouldn't cast aside for Red's amusement. I waited for the reply that kept not coming. The thought of his reading my letters stoked my pretensions; his very silence only confirmed my sense of the power of words. It was then too I decided that, when I grew up and started publishing novels, my ugly Scottish name—so common, smelling of peat fires and wet sheep fleece—wouldn't serve on the spine. I would adopt a pen name. I borrowed "Christopher Renquist" from the mailbox of a dentist down the street: it seemed a name with leather-bound editions in its bookcase and a pipe in its mouth. With my title page now readied, I was about to start on the novel itself when—after how long?—two letters arrived for me on the same day.

One was from the Ukrainian cook at camp, full of the same warm misspelled gush she'd served up all summer. A fat, plain, backcountry girl whom I loved to spend time with, she was so easy to impress, to confide in, to tease. I had never guessed that my imagined charms would outrun my ability to control their effect. Casually picking up the letter I had deliberately left on the hall table for them to read, my parents smiled at their son's precocious effect on women. I myself was of two minds, alternately flattered and saddened by my own talent to deceive.

The other letter was from Red. The silken writing paper had three strange blazer-blue symbols embossed at the top—his fraternity letters. It was brief, but it was *typed*. I postponed reading it as long as possible, no doubt to prolong a thrill as textured as the paper, as enigmatic as the Greek. Finally, I began. "Hi kid! Gee, it was sure great to hear from you, and all those funny stories. Hey, college life is really swell. You'll see. Well, I've got to get back to the grind. So long for now." I pored over it as years later I might a paragraph of Proust. I wanted to be alert to every nuance, every implication. Nothing would be lost on me. Almost at once, I had the letter by heart. Here were lines to be read between, sentiments suffused with feeling.

Still, my first impulse was to hide it. Hide it *from* my parents, yes, but also hide it *for* myself. I ran with the letter to the beach and, carefully calculating an imaginary line from my bedroom window to the gable of the lifeguard shack and beyond to a deserted stretch of sand, I buried it. As if to prove it truly a treasure I had laid up in my heart, I let a day go by before I snuck back to dig it up and read it again. The mental X that marked my spot was suddenly confused by new maps of seaweed and broken shell pointers. Was it three feet this way? Or two steps to the right? Had I forgotten about the night's high tide? Let's just leave me there, furiously digging, my eyes blind with tears.

Though I'd memorized what he'd written, I wanted the beloved's *writing*. I had put my trust in fetishes, in secrets. I had hidden something—my feelings—that I ought only to have disguised. A little later I had learned the lesson better. The hole I had dug in the sand—the sand itself having run through the hourglass of several years—was not as dark as the confessional's velvet gloom. If I felt at home there, it was because I was both reluctant believer and artful dodger. That is to say, I didn't want to "sin," but only to enjoy myself. A great part of the enjoyment was confessing the forbidden pleasures, because a great part of the pleasure lay in the subsequent fall from grace. This required that I find the dimmest priest. I got to know the sound of his particular mumble—or perhaps there was a slightly longer line in front of his box. But to pull the heavy curtain behind me and wait until his wooden slat slid open . . . that was the moment I most enjoyed. It was for that moment I had rehearsed my disguise.

The point was to confess my sin without actually naming it; to let the priest know enough to forgive me, but not enough to picture what I had actually been up to. "I have been impure in action twelve times." That formula seemed sufficient: both bland and correct, evasive yet official. Sometimes it prompted the priest's prying follow-up: "With yourself or with others?" But more often than not there was the unseen knowing nod, the sorry words of sympathetic disapproval, the routine vows and penances, the smug walk to the altar rail to kneel and ask forgiveness from a statue of some muscled martyr ecstatic with arrows. It was only when I had finally begun to sin in ways I couldn't think how to disguise that I lost my faith in both religion and language.

Of course, language had been my religion all along, and my faith in its powers of salvation was only temporarily shaken. In the end, it was merely the heavy burden of the church's authority that I had once and for all to shrug off. That was the easy part. So was Christopher Renquist's work-in-progress. Language and a literary ambition come with their own deadweight attached: the pressure every buoyant syllable of English puts on the tongue, the gravity with which every past achievement charges the imagination. But there was something more immediate, more intimate, and much heavier.

I cannot remember a moment of my life when I didn't know I was gay. My homosexuality was never a tendency, a phase, a discovery, a conversion, or a choice. Every instinct, every desire had from the start been directed that way. Like a drop of ink let fall into a glass of water, it was a small part of the whole, but imbued everything, was everywhere apparent. Still, at a certain time in your life, you become conscious of what you know. At about the same time I left the church I started being self-conscious about being gay. Can I make this generalization?—that a gay person is always more aware of his sexuality, and therefore may encounter it as a kind of *fate*, something apart from himself that also *is* himself. This in turn may lead him to hate or resent his sexuality, this possessive god within. For me, though, it was simply a fact, not a fate. It was a fact—like being a writer—that both signaled my difference from others and linked me to a secret band of brothers. And being conscious of this fact was less a problem than a challenge: how to act on it without being caught, how to live with it without being Known As Such. It's no wonder my first short story dealt with a single man who writes stories under another name—not a pseudonym but an allonym, the borrowed name of an actual person. It was my age of disguising.

There comes a time, however, when you have to tell. Admitting things to oneself is often difficult, but that sort of understanding—however tortured with tea and sympathy it was in the old novels—is usually reached privately and undramatically. Telling one's friends can be awkward, and occasionally frightens off one or two of them for good, but is rarely painful. The hardest disclosure—well, it was for me—is to one's parents. More than sibling or confidant, priest or teacher, they represent both authority and security. Their hold on one derives its force from history and myth: we have spent more time with them—emotional, physical time—than with anyone else, and in our minds we have made them over into figures larger, more loving and more threatening, than any mere human could be. And if there is a thorny hedge of denial around any topic between parent and child, it is sex. Neither can imagine that the other even *has* a sex life, and to talk about it—my father had never told me the facts of life, for instance—is an unbridgeable embarrassment.

For years I kept my secret to myself. Even if I could figure out how to put it, I dreaded hurting them and was afraid to defy them. In one scenario it was fire and brimstone; in another, tears and cold shoulders. It took me the longest time to face up to it. In fact, not until I had settled into a happy relationship with another man—I was in my late twenties—did I have the courage to tell them the truth. Half of it was Dutch courage. I was home on a visit. My youngest sister was still living at home, and she and my parents and I had all downed a couple of stiff drinks before dinner. By dessert time there was an odd and entirely uncharacteristic soul-baring atmosphere around the table. Each of us had decided to tell the others something we'd never told before. My sister disclosed I no longer remember what, but at the moment it seemed an intimate, probably racy secret. When she was finished, I took another long slug of red wine and pushed back my chair.

"Okay, my turn now. I think it's time I told you something about myself, something I've wanted to tell you for a long time, something very important to me."

I reached for my wineglass again. Over its rim I could see my mother's eyes narrowing.

"Don't bother," she said crisply. "I know what you're going to say."

Of course she knew. What else could she have concluded, years ago, from all those afternoons I'd spent listening to Brahms in my room while my father took my sister to the football game, from my wanting to play house with the neighborhood girls when I was young and later insisting on late-night pool parties with the classmates in my all-boys prep school, from acting out Eve Arden roles in our living room, from the too glamorous dates I found for the proms—oh, from hundreds of things done and not done, felt and not felt. My parents could see as well as I the texture of my life, like a cobweb on the lawn that if touched anywhere trembles all over, so tender that it feels everything. But what was more important even than my "orientation" was that it not be spoken about. That is what my mother's interruption meant: *Whatever you do, don't put it into words.*

In one sense, we were collaborators. Both sides had a stake in maintaining the ruse. They preferred silence. I preferred a manner-of-speaking. One hid the truth, the other disguised it. But wasn't my sudden insistence on coming out meant to subvert all that? And wasn't I making something more than a declaration? Wasn't I saying that from now on I would be in charge of my own life? It seems a basic desire, but how rarely granted to anyone! I meant to take control of a situation whose hypocrisy had been festering too long. Even more, I meant to change the way all of us "knew" what was what.

Keeping a secret is one way of sustaining the illusion of control; spilling that secret is the desire to manipulate what another knows and feels. We were a family, not of secrets exactly, but of a fearful incuriosity. Neither of my parents knew the names of their great-grandparents, or had any interest in finding them out. Here I was, nearly thirty years old, and I had no idea what all my father's business interests were or his income or his war record, what my mother's major in college was or if she'd ever been in love with anyone else. It's not just that we never discussed such things, we never even asked about them.

I was going to change all that with one simple sentence, as easily as unscrewing the cap from a pen. Not only was I going to force them to *know* about me, I was going to force them to talk about it. Not-speaking-about meant not-dealing-with. By putting it all into words I would move the matter to a higher plane than mere "knowing." From my sleeve of disguise, now turned inside out, I would pull the words that revealed and redeemed rather than belied and protected.

I swallowed the wine. I paused for dramatic effect. I looked at each in turn, and said in a flat tone that combined soulful resignation and matter-of-fact pride, "I'm gay." Let's just leave me there at the table, tears of relief in my eyes, tears of a different sort in my parents' eyes as I went on confessing my history, forcing them to listen, determined to reshape the facts of my life into a myth that would change them as well.

It wasn't until a year or so later that I discovered the truth. Or rather, a larger truth than the one I'd told that night. It was during a casual telephone conversation with my father. He asked what I was working on. In fact, I was writing a poem and needed a detail. I asked him if he remembered Dr. Schreiber. He did, and it was then he told me *his* secret.

Years before—I was a young graduate student at Yale then—I'd found myself curled up on the floor of the dining room in the little house I rented, wedged into a corner, sobbing, staring at the telephone on the floor beside me, waiting for it to ring, waiting for I didn't know who to call. A friend had happened by, easily sized up the situation, and suggested I check in with one of the psychiatrists at the University Health Service. Bursting out in tears, I'd picked up the phone and made an appointment.

In those days, a student was allowed ten free sessions with a staff psychiatrist, at the end of which you were either cured or referred elsewhere. I was assigned a young resident, and everything about him both prompted and confused my reason for being there. It was clear even to me that my motive in coming was to find some way of living with the fact that I was gay. Being gay was not itself the problem. Everything *else* was the problem—the pressures, the opprobrium, the future, the double life. I could manage being gay, but not the added burden of disguising it. And as soon as I walked into the consulting room, I knew there would be a new problem. My doctor was young, blond, handsome. His name was Will. He was, as it turned out, the older and better-looking brother of a movie actor who was starring as the heartthrob in that season's blockbuster. I fell for him at once.

"What do you think the problem is?" It was the second time he'd asked that question, and it finally stirred me from my daydream. Since I couldn't tell him that *he* was suddenly the problem, or stood in for what had always been the problem, I shrugged. I looked up his name in the faculty directory (his wife's name in parentheses beside his) and the address of his apartment complex in the suburbs. I took to driving out there, parking in the lot, and gazing up at his balcony—or at the baby-bucket in the backseat of his car. I was obsessed. By the tenth session I was in tears again, begging him to keep me. He consulted his supervisors, agreed to continue seeing me, and started smoking a pipe. Week after week, I came clean with him or lied—whatever I thought would deepen our intimacy. The purpose of the sessions was lost in this feverish new business of disguising my feelings. He came home from work later and later. I knew because I was already parked, with the vizor down, in a far corner of his lot. I once saw him arguing with his wife on their balcony. Another time I spent the night: my car had stalled. The sessions, too, seemed stalled. Getting the story out was hard, but at last he opened up. He began to tell me about his domineering father, his jealousy of his brother, all the time a new baby takes. By now I was smoking the pipe. I almost hated myself for what I was doing, but I was fascinated by the curl his story, like pipe smoke, was taking around the currents of my sympathy. I asked if we could talk about it all outside the office. Perhaps dinner? He'd phone next week? The transference was complete.

By which I mean—the call came soon—I was transferred to another doctor. Poor Will, having confessed, was yanked off the case, and it was suggested by his superior that I see someone named Dr. Schreiber. Of course I was crushed. But also intrigued by the fuss I had caused—and by the graybeard sitting like a pasha under a canopy of diplomas, as "distinguished," indeed as *admirable*, as my mother's classy fountain pen. *Schreiber*: his very name, the German word for "writer," betokened my ambition. We talked about "arrangements to be made," his fee and my life, and agreed on a schedule for both. Then, for nearly a year, we plunged back into my past, back to . . . well, to a happy childhood. That is to say, my memories were largely happy ones.

Oh, but how I hate to disappoint. I would zero in on anything I thought might accuse my young self of betraying its desires. I would renounce anyone—my parents, Red, Will—in order to make a new conquest, this time not someone to love, but someone to emulate. Our weekly hour seemed so fluent and worldly wise, as poised as any poet's stanza. The doctor's increasing silence only brightened my chatter. Perhaps he knew what he was doing. The more I carried on and tried to please, the more I grew convinced that my sexuality wasn't a choice—like pleasing—but a given, a fact, a discovery to be made of a treasure buried there from the start.

But even that wasn't right exactly. What it lacked was a body. So I began to alternate the shrink with the disco, the therapy of someone's Rush, the umpteenth round of "Smarty Pants," the floor full of cavaliers in designer jeans, each partnered by the trance he'd turned himself on to, by the glamour of a type he'd turned himself into: dropout honcho, wasted dopehead, guardsman with advanced degrees. Let's just leave me there, in the middle of the flickering dance floor, head thrown back to the singer's wailing promise of "what you've been waiting for."

The waiting seemed interminable. We'd been talking in circles for months. (It would take, by the way, another few years before I met the man whom I decided to spend the rest of my life with—a man now long since gone—and who soon gave me the courage to speak to my parents about being gay.) All that small talk while a fantasy undressed was getting nowhere. I told him so. He didn't seem offended. "Rejection especially tells us what we want, now doesn't it?" What did he mean? I was rejecting Schreiber, not the other way around. I walked out of his office for the last time late one stifling August afternoon. The night before, the disco's license had been revoked.

What I didn't know then, didn't know until that phone call to my father, is that after my first meeting with Dr. Schreiber *he* had telephoned my father. The deal had been that Yale would pay half his fee for our sessions and that I would pay the other half. I couldn't afford it, and had called my father to ask if he'd cover me. I told him I needed to see a therapist. He didn't ask why, and agreed at once to help. I told Schreiber to send his bill to me and my father would pay. That was that. But behind my back, to ensure that his fee would be fully taken care of, the doctor called my father to verify the payment plan and told him why I had sought professional help in the first place. He told him about Will. He told him what I had been disguising all those years.

In the years that passed between those two phone calls to my father—first Schreiber's and, years later, mine—he had never said a word, had borne his own disappointment or confusion in silence, had never confronted or accused or advised me. Only gradually did I realize how much I owed to my father's loving forbearance. But what first struck me, when I found out about that doctor's weasely call, was what a farce his betrayal now made of my brave, overrehearsed coming-out scene.

Whose secret, after all, had been revealed that night? What is the effect of telling someone a "secret" he already knows? And who precisely had been keeping the real secret all along? It seems to me now, so many years later (years even after my dear father's death), that I had been both right and wrong that night. Right, I guess, to bring things to the surface, though all it really occasioned was months of the kind of tense confrontations that Family Discussions so often become. Embolded by my own bravado, I overdid everything. I insisted that they not only know but accept, even applaud. They refused—silently; and the silence *after* a spoken revelation is even more maddening. I climbed onto one political hobbyhorse after another and charged the vanes of their resistance. And that too is how I went wrong: by my insistence on being *right*.

I look back on it ruefully. One's life comes to seem less and less individual, and the crises and battles of the past, the anguish and assertiveness, tend to blur. I'm no longer young, and not yet old. I'm not attractive, not ill, not hip, not angry, not hopeful. I don't dance. I don't march. And I don't have any secrets left. They are what I miss most. By making things impossible to overlook, coming out is the opposite of *hiding*. What I wanted, for the longest time after I forced the issue, was the opposite of *disguising*—which is, of course, nothing but another sort of disguise, something more subtle, more hesitant, more wistful, something with more soul and less willfulness.

It is while in such a mood that one takes up again an old school text. Late at night, in bed, with a book or my pen, I could trace other men's secrets. I'd look there for echoes of my own secrets, so long vanished into the thin air of honesty. The great poet Horace, for instance, gave me one cue. At the height of his career he was the most elegant and admired poet in Rome, and the emperor Augustus Caesar commissioned from him a fourth collection of odes.

The first poem in that book is addressed to Venus, the goddess of love, imploring her to leave him alone, to pay attention to the devotions of younger men. Horace was fifty—my own age as I write this—and he felt his erotic and romantic life was over. Yet the poem itself finds tears still left in the poet, like a buried secret, a hidden fountain. They were the same tears I suddenly found in my own eyes as I read the Latin—and I set about making a contemporary version of the old poem. I called it "Late Night Ode."

It's over, love. Look at me pushing fifty now,
    Hair like grave-grass growing in both ears,
The piles and boggy prostate, the crooked penis,
    The sour taste of each day's first lie,

And that recurrent dream of years ago pulling
    A swaying bead chain of moonlight,
Of slipping between the cool sheets of dark
    Along a body like my own, but blameless.

What good's my cut-glass conversation now,
    Now I'm so effortlessly vulgar and sad?
You get from life what you can shake from it?
    For me, it's g and t's all day and CNN.

Try the blond boychick lawyer, entry level
    At eighty grand, who pouts about the overtime,
Keeps Evian and a beeper in his locker at the gym,
    And hash in tinfoil under the office fern.

There's your hound from heaven, with buccaneer
    Curls and perfumed war paint on his nipples.
His answering machine always has room for one more
    Slurred, embarrassed call from you-know-who.

Some nights I've laughed so hard the tears
    Won't stop. Look at me now. Why *now*?
I long ago gave up pretending to believe
    Anyone's memory will give as good as it gets.

So why these stubborn tears? And why do I dream
  Almost every night of holding you again,
Or at least of diving after you, my long-gone,
  Through the bruised unbalanced waves?

I think back now to all my long-gones. I think back to Red. And to poor
Will. I think back on the men I've had secret crushes on and couldn't say anything to. And I remember those I could tell, or sort of tell. And I dream about
the three men whom I have loved most, love still, the men whom at the start
I kept secret from others because they had so changed my life. Each of these
men I have disguised in—or really, transformed into—poems in order to keep
hold of them. Like some minor god in an old myth, I've changed them back
into secrets. A poem needs disguises. It needs secrets. It thrives on the tension
between what is said and not said; it prefers the oblique, the implied, the
ironic, the suggestive; when it speaks, it wants you to lean forward a little to
overhear; it wants you to understand things only years later.

There's a stain I've just noticed here on the underside of the spread (I'm writing this in bed) that must be ink. It looks like a birthmark or puckered galaxy.
I shouldn't be using my fountain pen in bed at all. It's old-fashioned, and messy
to boot. How many times now have I fallen asleep still holding the thing and
by morning found it had spilled its secrets all over? Yes, its secrets. That's what
my fountain pen holds. It has drunk up all the slow-dripping sadness, engorged
itself with rapture and the grief that comes to. My pen is filled with a heady
elixir compounded of salt water and sweet fire, of heartsblood and aftermath,
of furtive arousals and a mirroring solitude, all blended to the tincture of time,
a cloudless midnight blue. When I hold the nib to my nose, I can smell it. It's
the smell as well on my fingers and inside the genie bottle of ink on my night-
stand. The smell of fresh bandages, wet leaves, quicksilver. It might as well be
the smell of memory itself. What may have begun as a hidden guilt eventually
surfaces as merely a memory, and we want to keep a few of them secret
because, in the end, memories seem to be our true, our only innocence.

4 . <u>C O M M O N P L A C E S</u>

?

?

?

?

I have from time to time kept both a notebook and a journal. They are very different things, as different as a recipe and the plat du jour. The one book I've scribbled in consistently, though, is my commonplace book, a sort of ledger of envies and delights. "By necessity, by proclivity,—and by delight, we all quote," says Emerson. But there is more to it than that. The sentences I hoard—to be literally figurative about it—are images. And as G. K. Chesterton once wrote: "The original quality in any man of imagination is imagery. It is a thing like the landscape of his dreams; the sort of world he would like to make or in which he would wish to wander; the strange flora and fauna of his own secret planet; the sort of thing he likes to think about." The bowerbird in me is forever collecting colored threads and mirror-shards to make a sort of world. My secret planet is populated by Diana Vreeland and Dwight Eisenhower and Yukio Mishima and Sergei Rachmaninoff and John Cage and Jean Henri Fabre and Dizzy Gillespie and Elizabeth Bowen and hundreds of others: a sort of Mad Hatter's tea party of brilliant conversationalists talking over and at odds with one another. I don't use their remarks in my poems; I sometimes quote from them in my prose. But for years now I've been collecting them. I collect them for their own sake. I collect to admire, not merely to appropriate. I collect phrases because of the way, in each, something is put that is both precise and surprising. Twice-distilled poems? No. But an abstract model for the poetic.

Perhaps one day I shall make a small book of them. Fifteen years ago, I would have included aphorisms of my own. (Here's one that comes to hand: "Memory's like a cherished old neighborhood. After a time, the wrong sort of people move in.") Today, phrase-making bores me. I had lists of words that intrigued me; catalogues of "other voices overheard" while poems by Crane or Stevens or Warren were read out to me after a dose of hashish; lists of ideas from Wilde or Proust or Valéry; bits clipped from newspapers are tipped in. Nowadays, the entries are less frequent, more bemused, less intimate. There's a recurring character, named X, to whom phrases happen. What follows are a few excerpts, more or less randomly chosen.

•

"Those who have free seats boo first." —Chinese saying

Thoreau, in his journals, on how hard it is to read a contemporary poet critically: "For, we are such a near and kind and knowing audience as he will never have again. We go within the fane of the temple, but posterity will have to stand without and consider the vast proportions and grandeur of the building."

An example of literalism. When Lord Cornbury opened the New York Assembly in 1702 in drag—in the style of Queen Anne, in fact—and was challenged, he is reported to have answered: "You are all very stupid people not to see the propriety of it all. In this place, and on this occasion, I represent a woman, and in all respects I ought to represent her as faithfully as I can."

• his squeeze-box
• but less of that anon

"For the last third of life there remains only work. It alone is always stimulating, rejuvenating, exciting and satisfying." —Käthe Kollwitz

"When the axe came into the forest, the trees said: the handle is one of us."
— Turkish saying

Apropos the work of older artists becoming more spare, it should be noted that this is not always obvious. *Parsifal* is the thinnest of RW's scores (in terms of printed bulk, that is).

- *frère-ennemi*
- *bel canto* > can belto
- Eadweard Muybridge sequential photographs > Egyptian two-dimensional figures
- X's ideas seem to have been lifted from fortune cookies
- *limae labor* (Horace), "the work of the file"
- scrape X off my shoes
- *bougereauté*

"All literature is to me me." — G. Stein

Van Eyck's motto: "As I can but not as I would."

"Il faut choisir: une chose ne peut pas être à la fois vraie et vraisemblable."
— Braque

12.ii.87. On Joyce Carol Oates's office door, she's taped up a card on which she's typed out this remark by Robt. Louis Stevenson: "To be idle requires a strong sense of personal identity."

On the overemphasis of clarity in writing: A. J. Liebling said the only way to make clear pea soup is to leave out the peas.

"Cinema is simply pieces of film put together in a manner that creates ideas and emotions." — Hitchcock

"Rome, Italy, is what happens when buildings last too long." — Andy Warhol

Ravel, on his critics: "Does it not occur to these people that I may be artificial by nature?"

"Verse that is too easie is like the tale of a rosted horse." — Gascoigne

On a postcard from the old, ailing Auden to a composer who'd asked him for a libretto: "Too sad to sing."

Hemingway said there are two ways to spend an evening. Get into your Buick, shut the windows, and sit near the exhaust. Or go to a cocktail party.

Frost said he was "content with the old-fashion way to be new."

The story is told — I think of Brahms — that the master was made to listen to a new score by a young composer. As he did, he kept raising his hat. The young man asked him why. "I'm just saying hello to old friends," he replied.

Told that a certain poem resembled an older poem, Allen Tate replied, "It had damn well better."

Poussin, from a letter to a friend, 1642: "The beautiful girls you will have seen at Nîmes will not, I am certain, delight your spirits less than the sight of the beautiful columns of the Maison Carrée, since the latter are only ancient copies of the former."

Fernando Pessoa's heteronyms: Alvaro de Campos, Ricardo Reis, Alberto Caeiro.

hanami: [the season of] cherry blossom viewing

Which mandarin has the longest fingernails?

• bread and circuses
• X's work is like a Grinling Gibbons carving
• mutton dressed as lamb

Coleridge described himself as a "library-cormorant."

Poe distinguishes between obscurity of expression and the expression of obscurity.

Du Bellay: "Rien ne dure au monde que le tourment."

"Res tene, verba sequentur." — Cato the Elder

Virgil Thomson, watching a beautiful woman walk toward him down Fifth Avenue, turned to his companion and whispered: "It's at times like this I wish I were . . . a lesbian."

Philip Sidney wanted from poetry a "heart-ravishing knowledge."

Mallarmé said that the French word for "day" sounded like night, and vice versa.

"Who plans suicide sitting in the sun?" — Elizabeth Smart

The Marquis de Sade is descended from the same family as Petrarch's Laura.

Paul noticed this bumper sticker on the L.A. Freeway yesterday: "The meek are contesting the will."

• sottocapi
• X is copperbottoming his career
• The Flat Earth Society

Dylan Thomas's blurb for Flann O'Brien's *At Swim-Two-Birds*: "This is just the book to give your sister if she's a loud, dirty, boozy girl."

On his passport, Stravinsky listed himself as "inventor of sounds."

Maria Tallchief, withdrawing from the New York City Ballet in 1965: "I don't mind being listed alphabetically, but I do mind being treated alphabetically."

"Outside of a dog, a book is man's best friend. Inside of a dog, it's too dark to read." — Groucho Marx

Emerson referred to the "Poetry of the Portfolio": "the work of persons who wrote for the relief of their own minds, and without thought of publication."

Klimt said that to write anything, even a short note, made him "seasick."

Lao-tzu: "The Way that can be spoken of is not the True Way."

- X got up on his hind legs and . . .
- X is filling a much-needed gap
- backbencher; ward-heeler
- *un mutilé de guerre*
- frog-marched

Optima dies prima fugit.

Motionless, deep in his mind lies the past the poet's forgotten,
Till some small experience wake it to life and a poem's begotten,
Words its presumptive primordia, Feeling its field of induction,
Meaning its pattern of growth determined during construction.
   —WHA, note in "New Year Letter"

"Some people think that luxury is the opposite of poverty. Not so. It is the opposite of vulgarity."—Coco Chanel

"Technique in art . . . has about the same value as technique in lovemaking. That is to say, heartfelt ineptitude has its appeal and so does heartless skill, but what you want is passionate virtuosity."—John Barth

"Exuberance is Beauty."—Blake

To the wounds of his victims Torquemada applied thistle poultices.

Euclid defined a point as having position but no magnitude.

Roethke had submitted "The Lost Son" to *Horizon*. Sonia Brownell (later Orwell) returned it with this remark: "It seemed to us that your poetry was in a way very American in that it just lacked that inspiration, inevitability or quintessence of writing and feeling that distinguishes good poetry from verse."

"Poets are jails. Works are the convicts who escape."—Cocteau, diary, 23.iii.53

11.xi.90. In line with Jane for a movie at MOMA. SM approaches, said he'd been at the NYU reading last week and been struck by my new Bishop poem. Did I remember the Cambridge reading of long ago? he asked. I did. Did I remember talking with Lowell about Bishop? I didn't—but he had been listening in. He overheard me asking Cal what might account for EB's popularity. "All the fags like her" was his answer.

Tom Paulin refers to an Irish word *thrawn* to mean a poetry or language where there's "something a bit difficult, a bit contorted," as in Donne or Hopkins or Browning (or Frost, he adds, and Hardy).

For the Greeks, memory was "the waker of longing."

Happiness is what I most know in life, but grief is what I best understand of it.

Harold Bloom: "My favorite prose sentence by Mr. Ezra Pound is in one of his published letters: 'All the Jew part of the Bible is black evil.' And they ask me to take that seriously as a Western mind."

"What constitutes adultery is not the hour which a woman gives her lover, but the night which she afterward spends with her husband."—George Sand

A British critic described Beverly Sills's voice, later in her career, as "part needle, part thread."

- rust-proof
- X has floured his sauce.
- the talking classes
- fan de siècle
- a slash of gin

The Japanese ideogram for "noise" is the ideogram for "woman" repeated three times.

"*All* must have prizes," said the Dodo.

Schoenberg's transcription of "The Emperor Waltz" for clarinet, violin, cello, and harmonium—an image for *translation* in general?

My old college teacher Elias Mengel once showed me his copy of Wallace Stevens's *Collected Poems*, which WS had inscribed: "Dear Elias: When I speak of the poem, or often when I speak of the poem, in this book, I mean not merely a literary form, but the brightest and most harmonious concept, or order, of life; and the references should be read with that in mind."

O. Wilde: "Only mediocrities develop."

Robert Pinget, on his own writing: "You might call it a kind of automatic writing carried out in a state of total consciousness. . . . I am now convinced that in a work of art we do not try to conjure up beauty or truth. We only have recourse to them—as to a subterfuge—in order to be able to go on breathing."

"I have played with quite a few musicians who weren't so good. But as long as they could hold their instruments correct, and display their willingness to play as best they could, I would look over their shoulders and see Joe Oliver and several other great masters from my hometown."—Louis Armstrong

Balanchine: "*Apollo* I look back on as a turning point of my life. In its discipline and restraint, in its sustained oneness of tone and feeling, the score was a revelation. It seemed to tell me that I could dare not to use everything, that I, too, could eliminate."

"The closer the look I take at a word, the greater the distance from which it looks back."—Karl Kraus

Freud on the surrealists (from the journal of Princess Marie Bonaparte):

"They send me all their productions. They think I approve what they write. But it isn't art."

The measure of a poem's "immortality" is the later life it has in other poems. Imitation, appropriation—dismemberment and regeneration—by new poets give the old poem its purchase on life.

Braque on Picasso: "He used to be a great artist, but now he's only a genius."

Andrew Lloyd Webber is reported to have once asked Alan Jay Lerner, "Why do people take an instant dislike to me?" Lerner replied: "It saves time."

Pope, on his *Brutus* (of which an outline and eight lines remain): "Though there is none of it writ as yet, what I look upon as more than half the work is already done, for 'tis all exactly planned."

"A book is never a masterpiece. It becomes one."—from the Goncourts' journal

- pompier
- Boot Hill
- majaism (Philip Levine's work?)
- X's poems are *objets de vertu*
- X's grasp exceeds his reach
- wings-and-flats
- Which is the quick brown fox and which the lazy dog?
- a musical term: the dragged glissando

Jean de Reszke's voice was described as having "le charme dans la force."

Age is a caricature of the self (or the self's body and features). To make someone look funny—or do I mean merely to make fun of someone?— make him look older.

About his wife, Camille, on her deathbed, Monet writes: "I found myself, without being able to help it, in a study of my beloved wife's face, systematically noting the colors."

Nietzsche held the "refinement of cruelty belongs to the springs of art."

"Tu nihil in magno doctus reprehendis Homero?" — Horace

Graham Greene said that for a writer success "is always temporary, success is only delayed failure. And it is complete."

The Count, in Castiglione's *Il Cortegiano*, on the ancients: "If we follow them of old time, we shall not follow them."

X is water under the burning bridge behind me.

X has written an unauthorized autobiography.

Mme. de Sévigné on sightseeing: "What I see tires me and what I don't see worries me."

Arthur Miller: "Just play the text, not what it reminds you of."

Walter Sickert, showing Denton Welch to the door: "You must come again when you have less time."

La Rochefoucauld said that the wish to be exclusively wise is very foolish.

Virgil Thomson said that opera is all about saying good-bye and ballet is all about saying hello.

Pascal: "The last thing you get to know is what should come first."

Nabokov, *Look at the Harlequins!* "In those days I seemed to have had two muses: the essential, hysterical, genuine one, who tortured me with elusive snatches of imagery and wrung her hands over my inability to appropriate the magic and madness offered me; and her apprentice, her palette girl and stand-in, a little logician, who stuffed the torn gaps left by her mistress with explanatory or meter-mending fillers which became more and more numerous the further I moved away from the initial, evanescent, savage perfection."

5 . TWENTY QUESTIONS

?

?

?

?

?

What exactly is "contemporary" poetry anyway?

Like the Beauty it often seems to have jilted, Contemporary Poetry is another of those concepts that is in the eye of the beholder. In the classroom it's used to distinguish whatever comes after Modern Poetry—itself usually meant to cover the heroic generation of poets, from Yeats and Eliot to Williams and Frost, who had braved the thorny perils of the Great War and Freud and Marx in order to kiss poetry awake from its languorous Victorian spell. In the main, we mean Modern to cover the period *entre deux guerres*. Contemporary Poetry, then, is everything since. Some would date it from 1945 or 1950, when the extraordinary generation of poets born in the mid-1920s came of age; others would start in 1960, by which time the publication of Robert Lowell's *Life Studies* and Allen Ginsberg's *Howl* had announced decisive new energies.

In another classroom down the hall, the argument is more wearily fastidious. Does *contemporary* mean, as some insist, only *living* poets? By that logic, the late Amy Clampitt, who was born in 1920 and whose first commercial book was published in 1983, is a contemporary, but Sylvia Plath or Anne Sexton, both born much after Clampitt and now dead for decades, are not. Perhaps a solution may be teased out of the term itself. *Temporal,* pertaining to, concerned with, or limited by time; so *con-temporary,* belonging to the same period of time. But *temporal,* by a slightly different etymology: pertaining to the temple of the skull. Is it too fanciful thereby to concoct *contemporary* as referring to what voices we all have in our heads?

Is it animal, vegetable, or mineral?

The poetry of Walt Whitman, the efflorescence of High Romanticism in American poetry, was a slow vegetable love of the nation and its possibilities. The modernists boldly mined the rich deposits of the language; the cold quartz gleam of their fragments can still blind. Contemporary poets, starting with Lowell and Ginsberg, unleashed a fierce, blood-hot force; you can feel it pacing back and forth in its cage of circumstance. The compulsion to rip out the living heart and plunge into its impacted horrors and empty chambers, to drink at the wateringhole of surrealism, to roar at the world and swallow the self: these are its animal appetites.

You make it sound like a zoo. Is it so frightful as all that?

No, it's more fun house than zoo. Its energies can frighten and amuse at the same time. Our poets over the past half-century have included every sort of two-headed moon-calf, bearded lady, pygmy groom, and formaldehyded baby. If anything can characterize the purposes of contemporary poetry it's the distorting mirror: traditions invoked and skewed, the self's dimensions bloated or attenuated.

Is there such as thing as a "period style"?

Absolutely, but what is more astonishing is our inability to notice it. Let's look backward—to, say, a book that sits on my shelf here, called *The Poets of Connecticut,* published in 1843. It includes forty-four poets, a few of them (history's average) reckonable, like Joel Barlow and John Trumbull and FitzGreen Halleck. I have no doubt that readers in 1843 appreciated the differences between these better poets and the likes of Ebenezer Mason or Emma Willard or Jesse Dow or Martha Day. What's more, they could hear how the sound and sensibilities of Asa Bolles and Prosper Wetmore (I choose the names at random from the anthology, as if from gravestones) differed one from the other. To our ears, of course, they all sound the same. Time has reduced all of them to the same faint, scratchy cylinder.

And today, when we delicately weigh in the pan of judgment the merits of W. S. Merwin's oracular whispers and John Ashbery's rambling discourse and James Merrill's fizzy formal cocktails, while we argue the advantages of Walcott's Caribbean accent or Creeley's clipped speech—what will the distant future be listening for? Won't they be listening for how much flatter, say, the twentieth century sounds when compared with the eighteenth, and not hear how different Dylan Thomas and Edward Thomas are, or James Wright and Charles Wright? Won't they be listening to the tidal flow of the demotic into verse, and be deaf to the quite distinctive uses it is put to by Robert Pinsky and Jorie Graham?

What of some finer distinctions among this half-century of contemporaries? Are there generations, movements, groups worth distinguishing among?

I'd count four mansions in the house of contemporary poetry, divided by decades. The first was the generation of Robert Lowell and Elizabeth Bishop, poets born in the teens who came of age in the dark shadow of the great modernists, poets who had read Eliot and Pound and Auden with the flush of first excitement and the desire both to emulate and inflect. There followed the remarkable generation of poets born between 1925 and 1930: the likes of John Ashbery, James Merrill, W. S. Merwin, A. R. Ammons, James Wright, Robert Creeley, Adrienne Rich, Galway Kinnell, Allen Ginsberg, John Hollander, Richard Howard, W. D. Snodgrass, Philip Levine, and so many others. This is a group that went to school during the Depression, apprenticed themselves to the New Critics and close reading, were thrown into World War II and a life afterward—uncrowded with poets—that allowed them to pursue individual voices. During the sixties and seventies, the strongest among them felt the pressure to change, to seek new figural dimensions for their work, new methods or refinements. As so often before, their experiments centered on voice: how to make the lyric voice heard. (I skip now over the 1930s. With a few notable exceptions—like Sylvia Plath, Mark Strand, and Charles Wright— genius seems to have flown by those born during this decade; something in the water supply perhaps?) The third group is the generation born between 1940 and 1945, the first raised to read "contemporary" poetry and to take their immediate predecessors as models. And finally, there are—there must be—poets born in the 1950s, just now establishing careers.

It goes without saying that each of these generations seems a bit paler than the one just ahead of it. Hindsight enhances.

Let's go back to that first generation of contemporaries. Why consider them contemporaries now? Most of them have been dead for decades.

Because they set the rules by which the game is still played. To write now in Eliot's world-weary wheeze, in Pound's manic shivers, in Stevens's boardroom fantasies, in Moore's twittering machine, would be merest pastiche. But the example, say, of Elizabeth Bishop's poems—written in the thirties and forties—still haunts the imagination of most writers today. Berryman, Jarrell, Warren, Roethke—each in his way left the poetry he had taken up a changed thing: its speech more intimate, its sights lowered, humbled by experience, its ambitions more horizontal than vertical, more eager to colonize a wide range of daily life, conscious and not, than to storm the heights of the sublime or the lower depths of history.

And which of those poets has come out on top?

Bishop by far. It's puzzling: anyone would have guessed that Lowell, the most prodigiously gifted poet of his generation and the most ambitious, would still set the standard. He was one of those rare poets of imperial imagination— Whitman was one, and Hart Crane—who found the poetry of his time brick and left it marble. Even discounting the ten-year slump that follows any celebrity's death, his reputation should long since by now have been securely polished and set up on the mantle. It's not been. That may have something to do with the way fashions in reading cross with historical circumstance. Lowell's bull-elephant poetic manner—granitic, complex, aggressive—has encountered a taste now for a milder, more domesticated style, with its shy wit or earnest epiphanies, and, at the same time, American politics settled into greedy ruts of quietude, so different from the tumultuous upheavals of Vietnam and the civil rights movement, convulsive national events that fired Lowell's imagination and forced his poems to seek out the electrical connections between the private life and the public life.

Poets with less natural talent—Randall Jarrell, say, or Allen Tate or Charles Olson—have faded as presences; so have poets like John Berryman, whose natural talent, it's now clear, was undone long before the end by (in his case) drink.

But Bishop . . .

What has sustained her reputation?

Certainly not the women's movement, and the now more widespread study of work by women. Bishop herself loathed that sort of isolation, and refused to allow her poems to be reprinted in any women-only anthology: she wanted to be judged against the best, all of them—which is, admirably, both a humble and an arrogant point of view.

Until recently, young readers came to Bishop's work almost furtively. Unlike Lowell, she was not—or not until late in her life—acclaimed and available, a powerful presence and constant literary resource. Now, of course, she is a part of every sort of curriculum and the subject of a burgeoning series of books and conferences and dissertations. But that wasn't true twenty years ago, maybe even ten years ago. Before then, each reader had to find Bishop in his or her own way; she had the advantage of being a cult figure, a special taste, an enabling rather than an overpowering model.

What is strange is how her influence—and thereby her power—has been felt in the literary culture. John Ashbery, James Merrill, and Mark Strand, for instance, have each claimed Bishop as his favorite poet and as an abiding influence on his work. Since each of them couldn't be more different from one another, how is it possible? The reason may lie in an observation Howard Moss once made to his notebook: "The truest changes in art are not changes of technique but of sensibility. And so the real pioneers are rarely recognized as such. They are too subtle to make good copy. Examples: Henry Green and Elizabeth Bishop." It may well be that what younger poets "got" from Bishop—and I use *got* in the sense of "understood"—is not a style to imitate but a part of themselves her example discovered for them and in them. Again, only a fool would set out (for very long, at any rate) to copy Bishop's obvious mannerisms—her hesitations and questions, say, or her odd hypnotic couplings: "awful but cheerful," "commerce and contemplation," "the somnambulist's brook," and so on. It's more likely that younger poets learned not what to put into a poem, but what to leave out. (Valéry once rightly said that a true poet is to be judged by what he excludes from his work.) It's likely that younger poets learned from Bishop not what to say, but where to look—or better, what not to overlook, least of all in themselves.

Should we believe everything we hear about her?

My own experience with Bishop has always run counter to the accepted opinions of her I'd heard about. That, say, she was a shy woman. I first encountered her after a reading she gave with James Merrill at the New York Y in 1973. As soon as the reading was over, I barged down front to pay my astonished respects. She had left her watch, it turned out, on the lectern, up on the stage. No sooner had I stuck my hand out than she barked at me—a total stranger—"Go up there and get my watch!"

Or the received opinion of her as a straightforward poet. I remember when her breathtaking poem "In the Waiting Room" first appeared in the *New Yorker*. Its casual reference to the February 1913 issue of *National Geographic* magazine, with its article about and pictures of Osa and Martin Johnson's African explorations, propelled the scholar in me (I was then a young assistant professor at Yale) to rush to the library stacks and retrieve the issue. Of course, there was no such article. When, a week later, I ran into her at a party in New York and told the story on myself, she looked puzzled and said, "Oh, it must have been the March issue." Like a fool, I went back to the library . . . No, not March either. Of course, her poetic point all along had been to make her poem sound as factual as possible; ruses rather than research are the trick for that effect.

Bishop always struck me, in other words, as a deceptively forceful, uncannily elusive poet. That's one reason, twenty years ago, I wrote a review of her *Geography III* that I modelled on Randall Jarrell's essay on Frost, which in its day so offended Frost readers by suggesting a much darker, troubled poet than people had been willing to read. It still seems to me that Bishop is the true successor to Frost in our American line of poets, and that the energies of her work are darkly instructive, a moral brooding. But nowadays I read her differently yet again. Not as the delicate observer, not as a moral teacher—but as something stranger yet. The opening lines of her poem called "Conversation" give me my lead: "The tumult in the heart / keeps asking questions. / And then it stops and undertakes to answer / in the same tone of voice. / No one could tell the difference." It is as if all the answers in her poems were further questions. Those poems now seem to me so abstract, haunted by lost possibilities and bad love. There's another line from the poem "Manuelzinho," just a single line about the accounts he presents the speaker: "Account books? They are Dream Books." So too are her collections. So many poems are set to moonlight, so many of them seem like waking dreams, troubled dreams. They remain achingly mysterious to me. It is this quality too that singles out a poet from her generation and—as time goes by—keeps her poems fresh. Like certain interpretations of the Bible, Bishop's work is continuous revelation. She changes as we do, and seems to provide what a poet needs, often without his knowing he needs it now. She prompts the younger poet into making decisions for himself and on his own—after having been startled or delighted or confused by something *she's* written, something that wasn't there the last time he read the same poem. *This* is how she influences us: by being a shifting ground that forces us to run for our lives. And by being an invisible presence over our shoulders when the work is done: severest critic and, therefore, ideal reader.

*Are you trying to say that, in some sense, the poet's muse is also his
ideal reader?*

The only fit audience for the poet is the dead, so why shouldn't the fiction of a muse be run together with the fiction of an ideal reader—that is to say, a heightened version of the poet's self? A convenient anecdotal version of that happened to me some years ago. Before retiring to a new home in England, W. H. Auden made a farewell reading tour of the States. When he came to Yale, where I was then a graduate student, there was a rapt and overflowing crowd in one of the college common rooms. I was lucky enough to get a seat— on the floor. It seemed the perfect position for the acolyte I then was (and in part remain); and besides, it gave me a view of Auden's ankles with their unmatched socks. I was spellbound by his reading, and afterward rushed up to ask him to inscribe my copy of his *Collected Poems.* He looked at me and said, "Turn around and bend over." What he wanted, of course, was to use my back as a desk. And he did. Auden was writing on my back! It wasn't until years later that I realized he's been doing that ever since. Smart poets let the masters keep writing by becoming desks for them, or using them as desks for ourselves. As a matter of fact, Auden's OED—a couple of volumes of which he used to sit on while he was writing—now sits by *my* desk.

And what of the next generation—those poets born in the twenties?

In retrospect, this extraordinary generation of poets can be seen to have divided itself, in ways that have little to do with style, into two camps: the poets of imagination, and the poets of experience. James Wright and W. S. Merwin are quintessentially poets of the imagination—and as often as not found the freshest springs of the imagination in the unconscious. During the 1960s and 1970s they dominated American poetry, and inspired less talented poets to ape their wholly original experiments: the bold attempt to escape the conventions of a consciously elaborated art, to let dissociated images do the work of a discursive rhetoric, to startle rather than convince. Another group of poets—not just Lowellian confessional poets like Anne Sexton and W. D. Snodgrass, but autobiographical poets like Frank O'Hara, Adrienne Rich, and James Merrill— was drawn by history and circumstance to find themselves in the world, to make the embattled consciousness and the personal voice the ground of a poetics.

What do the two camps have in common?

They have in common a process, a sort of coming-of-age rite that each poet of this generation seems to have undergone. They were all raised to have good manners. In what nowadays seems a condescending preface to her first book, Auden said of Adrienne Rich: "the poems a reader will encounter in this book are neatly and modestly dressed, speak quietly but do not mumble, respect their elders but are not cowed by them, and do not tell fibs: that, for a first volume, is a good deal." That was 1951, and Auden's understatement was no doubt meant as ironic praise. Still, his point could have been made of any first book by any leading member of this generation. Only later, and no doubt spurred by the example of Lowell's *Life Studies* and Ginsberg's *Howl*, did a profound skepticism about the "literary performance" set in. Richard Howard, in his classic study, *Alone With America*, has astutely suggested that our postwar poets deliberately went about losing their Midas touch: unschooled themselves, roughened or loosened the golden nets of their verse, preferring an impulsive voice to a chastened Style, the impression to the idea, a tentative flux to any ideal order.

What about the rise during this period of various subcategories—black poetry, feminist poetry, gay poetry?

As Cyril Connolly once wrote, the true writer has only one function: to write a masterpiece. Anything less—any partial appeal—marks that writer as bogus. What we saw during this period in our poetry (as in our politics) was the rise of new audiences, the creation of special-interest groups. This is really an extension of the regionalism that has pervaded American culture from the start. Unlike England or France, we have never had a single literary capital where tastes were formed and judgments made. There is as vigorous a tradition of California poets as of Southern poets; the Pacific Northwest and New York—little interested in each other—attract their own crowds. The same can be said of the new movements. Poetry has always been an ornament of enfranchisement. Weak poets play to the new crowd. (Maya Angelou's inauguration poem was an example of this. It astonished me—or would have astonished me, if I weren't by now used to this sort of ignorance—that the day after the ceremony the *New York Times* described Angelou's poem as "Whitmanesque," thereby confusing a catalogue with a checklist.) Strong poets continue to write masterpieces.

What of fashions in style? What is their shelf life these days?

About ten years, maybe a little longer. The craze for Merwin and Wright rode a wave with almost the exact trajectory and duration of the sixties counterculture. This is not to say that their poetry participated in or contributed to the anti-intellectualism of that era. Quite the contrary: their studied gestures, whatever their dreamy origins or effects, were deliberate literary maneuvers, as carefully plotted as any heroic couplet. In any case, by the mid-seventiess the style had pretty much exhausted its possibilities, and readers began casting around for new gods. They found John Ashbery. Or rather, they found his *Self-Portrait in a Convex Mirror* in 1976, which was awarded every major prize along with a celebrity unseen since *Life Studies* and Plath's *Ariel*. Ashbery found himself catapulted from obscurity to fame without any intervening period of patient understanding. His poems are autobiographical but obscure, cool but plangent, discursive but meandering or fabular. And they seemed to catch the temper of the times. Ashbery's poems concern themselves—in a wholly beguiling way—with how we try to make sense of things, dreams and desires and fantasies and memories, as well as "our daily quandary about food and the rent and bills to be paid." Everything is given equal value, equal time: the wittily flat surfaces of his poems slide our attention forward, even if the poem's nostalgias make us long to pause, reflect, abandon the poem for our own memories.

What happened to "the poetry scene" during the ascendancy of these poets?

By the 1970s, with the workshop baby boomers at large, there was a virtual explosion of interest in poetry. To judge by the claims for attention, by sheer bulk, there were—no, there *are* now—more poets, and more readers of poetry, than ever before. There are more magazines and books, readings and poetry-writing courses (at the local Y as well as the local U). Social fashions, followed by educational policies in the 1960s, sought to validate "creativity." The results were a general flattening, but also a general and confusing fluency. Perhaps babble is a better word for it, the blurring of tones, the loosening of rigorous standards. In a time when one is asked to admire a string-tied bundle of old newspapers at the Whitney Biennial, why shouldn't one take every heartcry-in-jagged-lines as a poem? It is no wonder sentimental, neo-con critics of poetry yearn for a golden age, when the old father by the hearth read to his children from a well-thumbed copy of Wordsworth. The holiness of the heart's affections has never seemed so distant, so desired.

Nonsense. There are more poets and readers today than ever, but the proportion of good poets and good readers is probably the same as it was a hundred or two hundred years ago. During the so-called golden age, Longfellow's *Hiawatha* was bought and read as a national epic, while Whitman's *Leaves of Grass* (published the same year, 1855) was ignored. Emily Dickinson's poems—which, along with Whitman's, are the grandest of the last century, and are now the measure of our imaginations—were not published at all. Time sorts these matters out. But to lament, as some critics do, that our day has witnessed the extinction of poetry's cultural authority is perhaps to have miscalculated poetry's ambitions and true purposes. Or to have read the wrong poets. Or to have read the right poets without reckoning their true power and place in our culture.

And what might that be?

There's a story I like that bears repeating. A few weeks before his death in 1977, Robert Lowell was in Moscow, on a State Department tour to urge the Soviet authorities to permit a freer exchange of poets between our two countries. The apparatchiks grumbled about ideology. "Art does not make peace," said Lowell. "Art *is* peace." It is a familiar and a tempting assertion, but, to some, a deeply suspect one. It has been used, after all, to sanction every extreme of subjectivity, every inward turning, every denial of the commonweal, every excess of originality, defiance, or obscurity. If one man's art, or one man's peace, is not everyman's, then what value is there in art? What, indeed, do words like *value* and *art* come to mean? There is an answer, a hard answer, that sweeps aside such worries. More eloquently than any other advocate, Harold Bloom has argued that poetry is precisely that sanction: the defense of the self against *everything*—ideology, history, nature, time, others, even against the self, and especially against "cultural authority"—that might destroy it. If poetry seems more difficult or eccentric these days than it did when either Longfellow or Whitman was writing, so are the conspiracies against the self.

What about the younger generations you mentioned?

I mentioned two groups: poets born in the forties and a still younger group born in the sixties. It's impossible to make generalizations about the latter—and nearly impossible to describe them. They will have published one or two books, and with rare exceptions a poet's characteristic strengths don't emerge clearly until a third or fourth book. That's how many collections most of the older group have by now published, so the landscape is a little more settled. These poets were raised amid the clamorous democracy of competing styles: Merwin, Ashbery, Rich, Merrill, Bishop, Lowell . . . a parade of models. The task this new generation had was to reject the bogus. The flotsam and jetsam that for years swirled around the New York School or the Beats had to be cleared away; the tedium of the workshop pretensions had to be outgrown.

It is interesting—purely from a sociological point of view—to note that these younger generations have many more strong women poets than earlier generations did. It may be merely coincidental—certainly no woman in the past was kept from writing poetry by any malign political conspiracy. It's just that the good women writers tended to be novelists rather than poets. Not today. Louise Glück, Sandra McPherson, Marilyn Hacker, the late Amy Clampitt, Jorie Graham, Rachel Hadas, Rita Dove, Gjertrud Schnackenberg, Mary Jo Salter, Ellen Bryant Voigt, Debora Greger, Thylias Moss, Heather McHugh, Alice Fulton, and many others—it's a crowded field.

You spoke earlier of a "period style." Is there one for these younger poets?

I'd suppose that the loose iambic pentameter line has come to prevail now among younger poets. Their poems are boxy or longish, but tend to rely on a regular line and on a quiet, conversational tone. Gone are the gimmicks of the past: the fragments splayed down the page, the absence of punctuation, and the like. It's a more sober poetry, perhaps a little grayer.

One has heard a good deal lately about the New Formalism. What's up?

It's one side of a wooden nickel. On one side, a real buffalo called L=A=N=G=U=A=G=E poetry, a frivolous exercise in nonsense. On the other, a big chief with a feather in his hair: the new formalists, who claim to be restoring traditional values to poetry. Where mindlessness was, there shall rigor be; where technical sloppiness was applauded, it shall be driven out with a crisp quatrain or brisk narrative. Their aims seem noble, and are narrow. Worse, their practice is rarely above the second-rate. It's not that they write in verse; it's that they write bad verse—exactly the sort of plodding, inaccurate lines that versifiers have been blamed for down the centuries. If only Pope were alive, here's a new *Dunciad* to be written! The parade of pasty, pinstripe formalists and preprogrammed L=A=N=G=U=A=G=E cyborgs, all slaves of a single idea, the feministas, hip-hop end men, hollow-voiced cliff dwellers from the Southwest, every Boston poet in a straight line so that they may pat each other on the back, East Village tyros . . . Lo! thy dread Empire, CHAOS! is restored.

But what of the connections between these generations, and between contemporary poetry and the American literary tradition?

You start more hares than I can jug. Let me take just one point of the many to be made on the subject, and use it to probe briefly the connections one *wants* to find. Americans remain a people without a history—as, say, a European would understand the term *history*. From the start, each of us has made himself or herself an "American." Each day we shed the past, the better to envision a future. Circumstances, events, patterns, theories—none of these are of great interest, because all are of little use. *Others* are in the way. Only nature satisfies—the great green maternal breast—because it allows us to impose our own image upon her. And only the self is a suitable subject for our poems. The lyric—the poetic embodiment of the self—is an American's instinctive choice—not epic or epistle or elegy. Why have our great wars passed unnoticed by our writers, but not our Western expanses, our forest wildernesses, our urban landscapes? It is no wonder Whitman's "Song of Myself" is the national anthem. It is no wonder Dickinson's hymns to unbelief are our religion.

Our contemporaries have continued their project. The obsession with the self's extremes—whether in Robert Lowell's patrician pathologies or Sylvia Plath's psychic screeds or Frank O'Hara's breezy diary entries—is a constant. The abiding desire for an individual "voice," a means to speak to the self under the guise of addressing others, is as urgent now as it was among the modernists. And the American impulse to dwell among untrodden ways is just as strong—even if since the 1940s "a natural state" has included drug trips and the therapist's couch.

Our poetry, in other words, remains the "self-evolving circle" Emerson said the life of any American is. And no matter how it's dressed, in a Dickinson's white shift or in the motorcycle jacket and hair mousse of the latest three-day wonder, our poetry remains the truest image of ourselves that we have: nowhere else do we speak to ourselves so passionately, so openly, so intimately.

6 . READING POPE

?

?

?

?

?

?

Epistle to Miss Blount, on her leaving the Town, after the Coronation

As some fond virgin, whom her mother's care
Drags from the town to wholsom country air,
Just when she learns to roll a melting eye,
And hear a spark, yet think no danger nigh;
From the dear man unwilling she must sever,
Yet takes one kiss before she parts for ever:
Thus from the world fair *Zephalinda* flew,
Saw others happy, and with sighs withdrew;
Not that their pleasures caus'd her discontent,
She sigh'd not that They stay'd, but that She went.
    She went, to plain-work, and to purling brooks,
Old-fashion'd halls, dull aunts, and croaking rooks,
She went from Op'ra, park, assembly, play,
To morning walks, and pray'rs three hours a day;

To pass her time 'twixt reading and Bohea,
To muse, and spill her solitary Tea,
Or o'er cold coffee trifle with a spoon,
Count the slow clock, and dine exact at noon;
Divert her eyes with pictures in the fire,
Hum half a tune, tell stories to the squire;
Up to her godly garret after sev'n,
There starve and pray, for that's the way to heav'n.
   Some Squire, perhaps, you take a delight to rack;
Whose game is Whisk, whose treat a toast in sack,
Who visits with a gun, presents you birds,
Then gives a smacking buss, and cries—No words!
Or with his hound comes hollowing from the stable,
Makes love with nods, and knees beneath a table;
Whose laughs are hearty, tho' his jests are coarse,
And loves you best of all things—but his horse.
   In some fair evening, on your elbow laid,
You dream of triumphs in the rural shade;
In pensive thought recall the fancy'd scene,
See Coronations rise on ev'ry green;
Before you pass th' imaginary sights
Of Lords, and Earls, and Dukes, and garter'd Knights;
While the spread Fan o'ershades your closing eyes;
Then give one flirt, and all the vision flies.
Thus vanish sceptres, coronets, and balls,
And leave you in lone woods, or empty walls.
   So when your slave, at some dear, idle time,
(Not plagu'd with headachs, or the want of rhime)
Stands in the streets, abstracted from the crew,
And while he seems to study, thinks of you:
Just when his fancy points your sprightly eyes,
Or sees the blush of soft *Parthenia* rise,
Gay pats my shoulder, and you vanish quite;
Streets, chairs, and coxcombs rush upon my sight;
Vext to be still in town, I knit my brow,
Look sow'r, and hum a tune—as you may now.

The older I get and the more I have read, the less do masterpieces appeal to me. The Great Books are an ideal school curriculum, and in old age may be a refuge from the vanities of the world, but they are not a companionable pleasure of one's middle years. I recommend those books and remember them and refer to them, but they are no longer on my night table. For the same reason that I now prefer Vuillard to Michelangelo, or Mendelssohn to Beethoven, so too do I prefer the sly lyric to the rigorous epic, the poem that amuses or touches to the one that scowls and stirs. I prefer the poem scaled to a human dimension, one that engages my own memories and desires. Even among the works of a very great poet like Alexander Pope—one of the half-dozen true masters of the art—I want now to single out a smaller, more tender, enchanting, and ultimately sad poem for special regard.

His "Epistle to Miss Blount, on her leaving the Town, after the Coronation" was written in 1714, and published three years later in his *Works*. When we pause to consider that in 1717 Pope was just twenty-nine, it may seem presumptuous of him to have issued a collected edition of his work—until we realize that the book includes such poems as his "Essay on Criticism," written when he was twenty-three, the sublime "Rape of the Lock," written at a mere twenty-six, and "Eloisa to Abelard," written at age twenty-eight. If he never quite lisped in numbers as he claimed, he undoubtedly remains the most astonishing prodigy of English poetry.

As a child, pampered by doting parents whose Catholicism and wealth he inherited, he showed—in Dr. Johnson's words—"remarkable gentleness and sweetness of disposition." Those qualities did not outlive childhood. As an adult, Pope seems to have been vain, petty, secretive, parsimonious, snobbish, greedy, and irascible. I wonder how much of this "bad character"—the very opposite of the sensible, modest, loyal persona of his poems—was the result of an unconscious self-hatred. He once described his own life as a "long disease." Literally, it was tuberculosis of the spine, resulting in a double curvature. It rendered him helpless, hunchbacked and repulsive. He was four foot six, "the little Alexander whom the women laugh at." In his life of Pope, Dr. Johnson describes him as "so weak as to stand in perpetual need of female attendance; extremely sensible of cold, so that he wore a kind of fur doublet under a shirt of a very coarse linen with fine sleeves. When he rose, he was invested in a bodice made of stiff canvas, being scarce able to hold himself erect till they were laced, and he then put on a flannel waistcoat. One side was contracted.

His legs were so slender, that he enlarged their bulk with three pair of stock-ings, which were drawn on and off by the maid; for he was not able to dress or undress himself, and neither went to bed nor rose without help. His weakness made it very difficult for him to be clean."

That, by this account, the poet was dependent on women, even as his weak-ness and deformity were exposed to them, has a haunting analogy in his emo-tional life. As a young man, Pope had met the Blount sisters, Teresa and Martha, daughters of a woman who had once been a neighbor of Pope's par-ents. He was infatuated with both the dark, sultry, sensuous Teresa and with her younger, blonde, shy, serious sister. He waited on them, lived to amuse them— Teresa especially. He settled annuities and a legacy on them, and eventually paid Teresa the compliment of writing one of his greatest poems for her, the "Epistle to a Lady." But it was all for nothing; they treated him like a pet mon-key. In one wrenching letter to Teresa—written in 1717, the same year his "Epistle to Miss Blount" appeared in print—he confessed his romantic frustra-tions: "Let me open my whole heart to you," he writes. "I have some times found myself inclined to be in love with you: and as I have reason to know from your Temper & Conduct how miserably I should be used in that circumstance, it is worth my while to avoid it: It is enough to be Disagreeable, without adding Fool to it, by constant Slavery. I have heard indeed of Women that have had a kindness for Men of my Make; but it has been after Enjoyment, never before; and I know to my Cost you have had no Taste of that Talent in me, which most Ladies would not only Like better, but Understand better, than any other I have." Of his first suggestion—that attractive women pursue gifted but ugly men—there is ample evidence. Chateaubriand comes to mind, whom Princess Lieven called a hunchback without the hump. Even so, women flocked to him, and the greatest beauty of her age, Madame Récamier, was his devoted mistress. Of Pope's second suggestion—that Teresa has ignored not just his person but the very genius that, beneath the body's disguise, is his true self—there is also melancholy evidence. A little after this letter, he sent Teresa a morocco-bound copy of his 1717 *Works*. He inscribed it with these lines:

This Book, which, like its Author, You
By the bare Outside only knew,
(Whatever was in either Good,
Not look'd in, or, not understood)

Comes, as the Writer did too long,
To be about you, right or wrong;
Neglected on your Chair to lie,
Nor raise a Thought, nor draw an Eye;
In peevish Fits to have you say,
See there! you're always in my Way!

But all this sadness lay ahead. In 1714, when Pope wrote his poem to Teresa Blount, he was still a sort of suitor, a man living in and for his hopes. Let's turn back now to the poem itself. In a letter to Pope, Jonathan Swift once noted that "you have been a writer of Letters almost from your infancy, and by your own confession had Schemes even then of Epistolary fame." The letters that brought him fame, of course, are his many verse epistles. His early "Epistle to Miss Blount" is the forerunner of those moral poems about friendship and virtue, modelled on Horace, that constitute his greatest achievement. So different in tone and address from the essay—or a poem like, say, his "Essay on Man"—the letter allows an intimacy and spontaneity that only help, by casually disguising them, to affirm its serious intentions. Most of us think our letters reveal more about us, because they plumb deeper, than conversation does. Dr. Johnson is less easily convinced: "Very few can boast of hearts which they dare lay open to themselves . . . and, certainly, what we hide from ourselves we do not show to our friends. There is, indeed, no transaction which offers stronger temptations to fallacy and sophistication than epistolary intercourse. In the eagerness of conversation the first emotions of the mind often burst out before they are considered; in the tumult of business, interest and passion have their genuine effect; but a friendly letter is a calm and deliberate performance, in the cool of leisure, in the stillness of solitude, and surely no man sits down to depreciate by design his own character." And what of Pope's poem? It has the tone of a letter, and is everywhere what Johnson calls a calm and deliberate performance. It is meant not to rush upon Teresa Blount's feelings but to describe them in such a way that he may identify with them. It may also reveal more about Pope himself than he may have intended.

The poem poses as a letter from the poet-in-town to his lady-in-the-country, but its real setting is the "dear, idle time" of a daydream. He imagines her to "hum half a tune," and he clearly means himself, in the poem's last line, to be humming the other half. This is a poem about harmony: the vexations of life yielding to an imaginative sympathy. Each is separated from what the poet would like to think of as the other's true desire. In his poem, each overlaps the other, and the two are joined. It is our thoughts, our "tunes," that unite us. Art may complete what life disrupts. This had been, all along, Pope's bittersweet self-delusion about Teresa Blount, and in this poem his effort to pretend that his ability to imagine will be crowned with success seems—because we know what humiliation ensued—almost unbearably poignant.

The poem's opening stanza is comprised of a single sentence, a single simile. (Its initial "As" finds an echo in the final stanza's "So"—a stanza also made of a single ten-line sentence.) The stanza swoons with barely repressed—or just awakening—sexuality. When Pope says of Zephalinda's friends and admirers that "their pleasures caus'd her discontent," he is referring not just to her envy but to her restlessness. (By extension, of course, Pope is describing his own feelings as well.) The next stanza, with its marvelous description of her routine in the country, is itself virtually a purling brook of words that signal repression: *plain, dull, cold, exact, godly*. Pope's exquisite satirical touch here must be what attracted T. S. Eliot to try the Popean couplets Pound excised from *The Waste Land*; but the tone remains—along with the image of trifling over cold coffee with one's spoon—in Eliot's best poem, "The Love Song of J. Alfred Prufrock." Poor Zephalinda's rural life here is just the opposite of Belinda's languid, exciting, treacherous life in "The Rape of the Lock," a poem written (or at least revised) in the same year. The bumptious Squire who replaces the city spark in her company is also, with his cry "No words!" the antitype of the poet. He loves you, says Pope to Teresa, "best of all things— but his horse." If you hear, as I do, "he's hoarse" there, then the echo implies that her oafish suitor cannot offer what (Pope would like to think) she most wants: the language of true seduction, the embodiment of love, the art of poetry. *Words* and distance make Pope more attractive than the awkward Squire who "makes love with nods, and knees beneath a table." By describing her desolate conditions, he suggests that he alone understands what her heart desires—wit, society, charm: everything, in short, that Pope, or his poetic voice, can provide. His muse of fire is its own sort of "spark." The three most seductive words in the language, undoubtedly, have always been not *I love you* but *I understand you*.

Since she cannot triumph in the rural shade, Pope imagines that in the rural shade she dreams of triumphs. Her daydream brings her memories to a more vivid life than her very surroundings. She teases them into thought only to dismiss them—with a "flirt," or flick of her fan. Pope's allusion to Prospero's dissolving pageant seems an intentional reference to the theatrical nature of the scene, and to Zephalinda's magical power. But of course the power is Pope's, and he next uses it gently. He puts himself in her circumstances: plagu'd and wanting and abstracted. What business seems to preoccupy him merely distracts him from his dreams of Zephalinda: his fancy has become his reality. And their interruption mirrors what happens to Zephalinda in the rural shade. His friend John Gay disturbs Pope's daydream, whereas Zephalinda wantonly makes her own vision fly. Perhaps Pope means to make Teresa seem the more willful. He had reason to. The poem's final rhyme itself contains Pope's own repressed anxiety. "As you may now" is a phrase that combines wishful thinking and uncertainty; he rhymes it with "I knit my brow."

"He used almost always the same fabric of verse," said Johnson. Indeed, Pope may be said to have perfected the heroic couplet. Yet isn't that very perfection a sort of limitation? It tends to lend the same tone and weight to everything. It concentrates, but narrows. It creates the vertiginous effects of balance and contrast, but is always pushing the lines from behind toward irony. It creates expectations that can be cleverly satisfied or upended, but tends to finesse the same tricks over and over. I say all this not to criticize Pope's technique—though I would acknowledge the drawbacks—but to praise his constant invention and flexibility, that astonishing way he has of making a line, or a set of lines, so expressive. My mind's ear links him in this regard to a poet most readers would wrongly think his opposite: Walt Whitman, who perfected the free verse line. Both poets make remarkable use of detail—Whitman, to contract and shape his line, which is always bulging outward; Pope, to expand and vary his line, whose instinct is to turn back in on itself. Whitman could make a scene, and sometimes a short story, out of each line in any of his catalogues:

The pure contralto sings in the organ loft,
The carpenter dresses his plank, the tongue of his foreplane whistles its
    wild ascending lisp,
The married and unmarried children ride home to their Thanksgiving
    dinner,
The pilot seizes the king-pin, he heaves down with a strong arm,

The mate stands braced in the whale-boat, lance and harpoon are
   ready,
The duck-shooter walks by silent and cautious stretches,
The deacons are ordain'd with cross'd hands at the altar,
The spinning-girl retreats and advances to the hum of the big wheel.

In his "Epistle to Miss Blount," Pope too lavishes detail; some lines have as much as any chapter in a Fielding novel. His descriptive and narrative genius is self-evident in this poem, but note his dramatic panache. "From the dear man unwilling she must sever"—one hears in that phrase "dear man" Zephalinda's own account of him to another lady. "And dine exact at noon"—one hears the dull aunt's pinched reminder. "And loves you best of all things—but his horse"—one hears Pope's mocking quotation.

What continually draws me to this poem is less its consummate art, its shrewd observations, its elegant stratagems, than the fact that all this art—each layer applied with the most delicate touch—failed. That failure only adds to the poem's melancholy pavane of crossed desires. Even without bringing a little biography to bear on the poem, we can read a larger perspective into it. I return to my earlier observation about avoiding the grandiose. The mighty themes can be so deftly treated in miniature. Isn't Pope's poem, after all, its own ironic *Paradise Lost*? In her Edenic garden world, Zephalinda innocently thinks she has lost the fallen world of town life, its gaiety, its dashing beaux and glamorous power. In his hellish city, plagued with headaches and noise and confusion, the poet knows he has lost his heart and fears he has lost its mistress, the beautiful girl. Both are unconsciously mourning their youth. That dull aunt and coarse Squire stand in as parodies of what the fair Zephalinda and the witty Pope will become. Perhaps Pope's genius in part lies in his having written a poem that, while hiding his heart from himself, has laid it open to us.

7 . ASPECTS OF "BATTLE-PIECE"

?

?

?

?

?

?

?

How, after all, is one to *read* a difficult modern poem? Where to start, what to bring, how to be sure? All the odds seem stacked in the poet's favor. I have heard people complain at poetry readings about the introductory remarks the poet may make on stage, setting up the circumstances of a poem's composition, its recurrent themes, its links with his other work. Why don't they ever put that sort of information in their books? an audience will ask. No artist ever does. He or she writes the scripture, and readers supply the midrash. Poems create and become their readings. There are times when the whole business seems a battle. The poet advances, armored and ornamented, gleaming and impenetrable. The foot soldier reader has a quiver filled with other poems, historical facts, inspired guesses.

Let me take as an example a poem that is itself about a battle. Or worse, about a painting of a battle, twice removed from the obvious. The poem is by Ben Belitt, who was born in New York City in 1911. Throughout his career as both poet and translator, he has been a remote, unfashionable figure, musing the obscure, given to high romantic gestures.

The poem is called "Battle-Piece." Its first appearance in a book was as part of his 1964 selected poems, *The Enemy Joy*, and a slightly revised version is included in his 1986 selected poems, *Possessions*.

Battle-Piece
(Uccello's "Battaglia di San Romano")

1. *After Uccello*

I have fought that battle in heraldic panels
Bitten in leathers, in Uccello's image,
Under the poising and the leveling lances
Crossing the visors and trumpets.
                I have seen,
In a hedgehog's vigil, ceremonious slaughter:
Halberd on battle-mace, crossbows tight on their jesses
With a hawk's extension, the rider's face
Bowed to his horse's mane under favors and feathers,
His profile naked to hazard in a locust's weight of armor.

What the fighting portended,
Or how, in a spoiled light, that leaden
Discomfiture darkened our spearpoints, the guidons
Failed on their silks, and the drum-skin's hoop grew tauter,
No one remembers.
            The maps and the outriders
Gave us no notice. The champion,
Sighting his lance's length in an umber perspective,
Awaited some sunburst to blazon that burden of armor
And interpret the contest's directive.
                Nothing responded.

2. *Another Part of the Field*

An unsuitable landscape, surely.
            Commanded
And chosen at once; inhuman and intimate, fated,
Familiar:

the light of apocalypse
Forced through the smoke of burning-glass,
Bitumen and nimbus together.
                    In the distance,
The hearth-beds of millet in a harrowed and featureless
Valley, the brand of the husbandmen's furrow,
Rose vertical.
                    Pomegranates reddened
The leafage—an eclipse's corona—yet the season
Was iron: a furnace's floor where no holocaust was:

And the time was Armageddon.

3. *Encounter*

The spur spins. The contender
Spins on the cinch's wheel of his saddle.
                    He measures necessity
With a pikestaff's haft, from his wish's circumference
To the center of violence.
                    Fatality flows
Down his pikestaff's length
To the curve of his bannerol. He touches the barb
To his pulses, steadies
The shaft on a corselet of nerves.
                    And is ready.
While that antagonist
On the belled Arabian crop of his stallion,
In a turban's swathe, his lance
On the pin of his elbow like the hub of a compass,
Forces mortality's sweat drop.

The spur spins, the contender
Spins on the dial of his saddle:
                    And the contest begins.

4. A Reading of Entrails

When the omens were served, we withdrew
To a higher position.
            We prepared for the reading of entrails.

We saw that the mottoes were struck
On a grave-keeper's cradle-song. The champion's
Shock on the champion, the decorum of armies,
The breaching of metal and adamant, breast-plate and barbican,
Were one to the sybil.
            The portent that orders all circumstance
Descends in a bloodbath, and legend is changed into chance.

But a legend was served!
            Whatever the omens portended
Or the weapon sought to refine to its satisfaction—
The bowmen debouched in the appointed valley,
The paladin's silks went up with the angry devices,
Emblem and ikon yellowed the embroidered borders,
Defender measured the field with the defended,
And all was ordered
As in a decoration by Uccello:

A foreground of horses:
            turquoise and cinnamon shod
With a jeweler's crescent; the straining albino,
His contemplative chessman's head in his bridle's rosette
Calm in the contact of riders.
            A navy of javelins
On the overturned horses—a carousel's
Splintered rotations:
            the field of the wilderness cinder
Fixed in its fated relations like an armorer's fable:
The House of the Rod and the Water-Bow, the Cresset, the Sheaf
    and the Gryphon—

The cinquefoil thicket laced with a pollen of poppies

The dismounted anonymous god in the goldleaf rubble—

And circling him there, on the broken lunette of his shield:
Three hares
      and a greyhound pursuing
            and the invisible thong of the snare.

5. *Festival of Anger*

One, with a trident, in the stable's
Ammoniac dung waits for the bluefly's epiphany; one
Turns from the watery burnish, the millennial
Barrow that honors a monster,
And enters a labyrinth; one, in a havoc of horses,
Harrows the world's rage with his lance's point
For a chapel, a chalice, the cannibal kiss of a brother.

Fighters in the blood, contenders
Antlered or garlanded, horned and necessitous ones—
Old changelings of the gorged heart of the toad
Who come by ways as desperate as this
To work in the breastbone and whiten the cicatrix:
However we sham or subvert the indifferent disaster
Or give the ungratified godhead of the scourge
The service of the sedulous offender,
Your angers are festive!

           Yours but to touch
The tinder to the tinder, the inexpressive
Desert adamant that hardens its venom
In the forge of the cactus,
And has no thought of sacrilege or pardons,
Incense, oblations, or talismanic letters:
           that breaks

The providential fountain from the stone
And looks like history or hope, but takes
A moment's inadvertence for its own.

I would fight that battle after the battle,
Inward and naked, after the outward
Packs like a weaver's spindle or poises like a picture
Baroque with the ceremonious violence of the shuttle,
The pencil, the burin, the matched and extortionate word—
The battle of the monster and the mothers
That no contender wages for a legend
At a charmed lake's bottom;
                              where nothing moves, but the imagining
Begetter and the habitual figures of his quarrel—
Who sees, beyond the landscape of surrender,
The pomegranates redden in a pomp of laurel,
The furrow blazing like a revelation—

And circling him there, still placeless and unimagined,
Three hares
            and a greyhound pursuing
                        and the invisible thong of the snare.

Even as the word *piece* has both a military usage (firearm or fortress) and an aesthetic one (composition or work of art), so too the more specific *battle-piece* is the proper term for either a pictorial or literary description of a battle. Belitt's poem rides grandly between the two. Given the vivid colors of his diction, the thick impasto of his syntax, it is surprising that he has not more often turned to art objects as poem subjects. Perhaps his own style is so strong as to be impatient with any mediated vision. In any case, it seems best to think of this ekphrasis as another of Belitt's translations. In the matter of translation, he holds with Coleridge's imagining man who "dissolves, dissipates, diffuses" in order to create anew. In the note to his translation of Lorca's *Poet in New York*, Belitt asserts "the translator is at liberty to contemplate the universe of a given poem [here read 'painting'] as its creator originally contemplated the universe of his given experience—not as a datum substantively present in the nature of things, but as a precarious search for exactitudes, correspondences, analogies which will mirror their model only in flashes, and which will demonstrate nothing so much as its partial knowability in the end."

At the outset we're parenthetically informed that the poem is based on, and pays homage to, Uccello's *Battaglia di San Romano*. But that general title refers to three different paintings, commissioned in the mid-1450s by Cosimo de Medici for a ground-floor room in his palace on the Via Larga to commemorate the Florentine victory a quarter-century earlier at San Romano. The three panel paintings, each about ten feet by six and placed in gilded woodwork high above the floor, were these: on the left, *Niccolò da Tolentino Directing the Battle of San Romano* (now in London's National Gallery), in the center, *The Unhorsing of Bernardino della Carda* (now in the Uffizi), and on the right, *Michelotto Attendoli Leading the Attack on the Sienese Rear-Guard* (now in the Louvre). As we read through Belitt's poem, it becomes clear that he had the Uffizi picture in his mind's eye, though details may have been drawn as well from its scattered companions, and in spite of the theatrical impression the poem gives not of merely tracing a picture's outlines but of itself creating before our eyes a dramatic history and moral significance.

"What the fighting portended . . . No one remembers." But, of course, we do. In the wars between Florence and Milan, the Duke of Milan had enlisted Siena as an ally, and by April of 1432 under the command of the *condottiere* Bernardino della Carda, the Sienese army had menacingly captured strongholds right up to the Elsa valley. The Florentine commander, Michelotto Attendoli da Cottignola, fallen into disfavor, was replaced by Niccolò da Tolentino, whose prowess at once began to stem the enemy's advance. In June of that year, a now overconfident Niccolò, planning to join up with Michelotto's main force but neglecting to communicate properly, set out with a small band of horsemen and accidentally encountered the Sienese army in the Arno valley near the tower of San Romano. He dispatched a message to Michelotto, turned to meet the Sienese, and for eight exhausting hours held his ground against great odds. At the desperate moment, Michelotto and his troops arrived, clinching a victory. And for long after the deaths of the participants, what came to be known as the Rout of San Romano remained a Florentine victory, having passed from memory into legend.

For a battle-piece, Uccello's picture seems remarkably calm and ordered. In all three panels there is only one human casualty—though the dead or dying horses, as Picasso knew, can terrify. This is more a tournament than a combat. And in fact, as Machiavelli wrote, "the wars in Italy were entered into without fear, waged without danger and ended without loss." So too has art, like memory, aggrandized a dusty skirmish. The nasty business has been ennobled with the plumes and crests and gold trappings of a fable or dreamworld.

Why do certain subjects even within the ekphrastic tradition—a particular painter, these exact motifs—attract certain poets? Curiously, opinions that swirled around the fifteenth-century artist have been those most often echoed in the hesitant critical reception of Belitt's own work. Vasari wrote of Paolo Uccello that "he was endowed by nature with a discriminating and subtle mind, but he found pleasure only in exploring certain difficult, or rather impossible, problems of perspective." He neglected the human figure, could not impart a required softness and harmony, ignored the rules of consistent coloring, so that his fields were blue and cities red. His close friend Donatello complained, "Ah Paolo, this perspective of yours makes you neglect what we know for what we don't know." Marcel Schwob, on the other hand, in one of his 1896 *Vies imaginaires*, likened Uccello to an alchemist who "believed he could transmute all lines into one ideal aspect. He sought to envision the created universe as it was reflected in the eye of God, who sees all forms springing up from a complex center." Imagining the painter's death, Schwob asks us to come upon the body: "Tightly clasped in his hand was a small disc of parchment covered with interlacing lines that led from the center to the circumference and returned from the circumference to the center."

Belitt's first composition to attract attention was a story entitled "Mended Armor." During his senior year at Lynchburg High, he was called to Charlottesville to read it in public, before a diorama of Raphael's *School of Athens*. The echo of "mended armor" is apt: his widowed mother had remarried a Virginia tailor and was thereby able to remove her three children from the orphanage and restore them to a home. That orphanage—the Hebrew Orphan Asylum in New York City, where he spent the crucial years of his childhood—Belitt remembers in military metaphors. "My childhood," he writes, in

"From the Bookless World: A Memoir," "was a surrogate world of the parade field, the public 'asylum,' the institutional regimen, without possessions or portfolio." (Not perhaps by coincidence, his book *Possessions* is what his art has since collected from his life.) His inheritance was "a Poetic of Orphanage which has served me as both a paradigm for the military life, with its massive regression to Booklessness, and a tutelary theme for my work as a whole."

His early undergraduate poems, written under the spell of Keats and Housman and Elinor Wylie, set about "turning chaos into epigram, and giving me a scrubbed sense of placement—that bonding of ego with the intoxicating materiality of language that turns discourse skeletal as well as magisterial." The lush plangencies of Keatsian pastoral helped him to this oedipal idyll: the union of self and mother tongue, haunted by a stern paternal ghost of reason. His asylum was no refuge. The image of the garden was an Eden of Imagination and the Past. (Perhaps his five-decade-long association with Bennington College was his literal garden.) But the military camp was there all along too, the parallel and opposing figure for this "antipodal man." This is the bookless, brutalizing world, fallen nature, masculine and overbearing. His 1943 prose meditation on life in an army training camp, "School of the Soldier" (published in a 1949 issue of the *Quarterly Review of Literature*), is the best gloss of this strain in his work, the dark side of his imagination. "It is in the waste of our wills," he says there, "that our violence begins, and our innocence, and our guilt." The routine of orders and drills has "a ceremonial characterlessness, a lunatic void . . . 'pure act,' " and action disallows the word, the verbal, the imaginative. Each recruit was merely an instrument, "a killing tool, bladed and hafted for the fist of an event which would in time make real our function." Going back still further, in Belitt's first book, *The Five-Fold Mesh*, a sequence of five sonnets from 1934 called "In Time of Armament" stiffly addresses our "inherited hungers" for bloodletting, and history's "new stratagems of terror." As in "Battle-Piece," the poet traces these conflicts back to "the medium of the personal will," and wants to prove that "Through all the forfeits of our innocence, / Our blood enacts a ritual of wonder."

In one of Belitt's best-known poems, "The Orange Tree"—a poem usually, and somewhat reductively, read as his *ars poetica*—his conceit works up the contrast between excess and essence, "armature" and "spirit." "The tree in the tree" is the ghost in this machine. On the one hand, we are given images of forge and hammer, holocaust and knife; on the other, sunburst and jewel, heaven and its epiphany. But the more often I read the poem the more I wonder if "to live in the spirit" for Belitt doesn't mean an "unbroken descent": to stay on the cutting edge as it divides rind from flesh. As it cuts, the knife joins. To "pare an orange" is to keep its *pair* of contending qualities: *to blazon that burden of armor.* As he puts it in another poem, "Armageddons, gardens . . . / The equivocal vision of judgment concealed in a parable." *Garden,* in fact, is embedded in *Armageddon.*

The text of "Battle-Piece" as it appears in *Possessions* is slightly different from its original version in *The Enemy Joy,* published in 1964. The real difference, though, is context. All during his career, Belitt's new poems have each been exuded from earlier work. His books, too, build outward; like tree rings, the latest section invariably faces outward toward the reader and inward toward diminishing but crucial selections from previous books. *The Enemy Joy* is divided into three parts: the new, titular group, a selection from *Wilderness Stair,* then nine poems from *The Five-Fold Mesh,* ending—in a gesture to emphasize the enfolding mesh of the collection—with the early poem that gives the entire new book its name, "The Enemy Joy." ("She sang the enemy joy as if it were grief," Belitt says of his emblematic bird in that poem.)

Part 1 is further divided into three sections: "Single Song," "A Sleep for the Lions," and "A Reading of Entrails." *Singing, dreaming, reading:* three modes of interpretation, or, in reverse, the three stages of conjuring a poem. The general title for the third section, "A Reading of Entrails," is the subtitle for part 4 of "Battle-Piece" itself—a sign again of how interconnected the parts of the Belitt book are. These entrails are a trail-in, a reading of the self. There are, appropriately, only three poems in this group—"Lives of Mrs. Gale," "The Lightning-Rod Man," and the first, shorter version of "The Orphaning." It might have been fanciful to construe these three poems as Mother, Father, and Child, if this triangulated obsession did not everywhere haunt Belitt's imagination. The series of "sorrowing women" and of despotic or idealized fathers runs straight through *Possessions. The Enemy Joy,* in fact, is dedicated to Belitt's father (his stepfather, I presume, not his natural father, who died in 1918), and the book's epigraph is this pair of lines from his poem "Karamazov," first published in *Wilderness Stair:* "How we squandered that ruin of fathers, / And how the inexhaustible fathers restore us!" "Karamazov" is a poem of violent abundance, and concludes with an image that in part anticipates "Battle-Piece," itself a poem about fathers: "A rider approached upon the inquisitor's errand, / Bearing the pardon that murders, and the murder that pardons."

The middle section of new poems in *The Enemy Joy*, subtitled "A Sleep for the Lions," has just two long poems in it, "Andaluz" and "Battle-Piece." Like Elizabeth Bishop's, Belitt's temperament has always shuttled between hemispheres of desire, North and South, Mexico and Vermont. In this section, we are south, a Mediterranean world at once sensuous, hieratic, and mythic—and slightly skewed: Moorish Spain, a nearly medieval Italy. "Andaluz" is the maternal side of this matched set of poems (each has five parts, and there are corresponding metaphors and allusions), its gauzy "Kingdom of Nuance," florid, enchanted, the verse lines shortened and softened. "Battle-Piece" is its harsher, masculine mate, its opposite number.

"C'est le propre de la peinture d'Uccello de ne pouvoir être décrite et définie avec des mots. On dirait simplement, et avec raison, que jamais peut-être un peintre n'a su mieux qu'Uccello ce qu'était la peinture en dehors de toutes autres considérations. Un lyrisme purement pictural, une puissance et une émotion également et uniquement picturales."—Philippe Soupault.

Belitt begins not by describing or defining but by dramatizing. In the phrase "After Uccello," *after* means *in the name of*. He will not follow the painter, but outdo him. We start with the self, a character, a voice: "I have fought that battle in heraldic panels." If we are initially led to expect a dramatic monologue, it will be eventually made clear that this gambit—like Whitman's "I am the man. I suffered. I was there."—instead signals an identification. This speaker is not, as he might be in another sort of poem, some obscured, lance-bearing foot soldier to the left rear of the ensemble. The poet himself, literally enraptured by the picture, is speaking—on his own, but as if a participant. Like the "eye" on its first encounter with the picture, the "I" is expropriated by the scene of battle. The pronoun later broadens: "*our* spearpoints," "Gave *us* no notion." But this is designed only to heighten what Roland Barthes once termed "the real-effect." Later in the poem, the "we" will yield again to the "I," in fact to the very opening itself: "I would fight that battle," the speaker says in the poem's last part. This later echo clarifies the true drama at the start. But for the moment the reader is left uncertain amid the swirl of details both rich and strange.

What in another poem, "The Loco-Bird," he names as "my need / for the marvelous" is everywhere apparent in the costume drama of the opening stanzas. Within the stately procession of blank verse lines is "confinement's opposite angel, overplus." The heraldic idiom here has been borrowed from labels in the museum's Hall of Armor: *visors, halberd, battle-mace, crossbows, jesses, guidons*. Clashing with these are self-consciously modern figures like "a spoiled light." Each of the first three stanzas is a single sinuous sentence; the first stanza, with three sentences, is both uncertain and decisive. Contrasts abound: the natural world (hedgehog, locust, horse) and the ceremonial "leaden / Discomfiture"; the naked profile and the weight of armor; "an umber perspective" and the awaited sunburst. What we have, then, in a word, is Belitt's style itself.

The poem's first three parts "read" the painting in terms of the observing eye. At first, the foreground's welter of figures and gear, of color both dimmed and ornate, commands attention. Next, the eye would, and the poem does, move to the background, with Belitt's Shakespearean stage direction "Another Part of the Field." Through a grid of lances that directs the eye around the picture's geometries, we recede from the battlefield to the farmed fields and distant doings. Then, with "Encounter," the poem's third part, we return to the dominant figures in the scene, the two duelling paladins. These three parts constitute the first, or more literal, half of the poem. The second half, or parts 4 and 5, figure forth the poet's meditation, his trails-inward. But even Belitt's descriptions of Uccello's work are highly stylized, febrile and evasive, private emphases bestowed, interesting details—what of those six tiny peasants toward the top who seem calmly to be harvesting grapes?—ignored. And throughout he is little concerned with Uccello's technique or modelling, with the famed perspectives or subsidiary figures, or the sculptural rendering of horses and armor, or the role of the lances and armor as definitions of and guides to the planes of pictorial space. It is as if, right from the start, the picture serves only to remind Belitt of something else—something evoked by the painting but independent of it.

The first part of the poem ends with "Nothing responded." In other words, there are no correspondences in the confusion. But in the second part, the poet starts to step back, to take a more general view and pass judgment on this "unsuitable landscape."

> Commanded
> And chosen at once; inhuman and intimate, fated,
> Familiar:
> the light of apocalypse
> Forced through the smoke of a burning-glass,
> Bitumen and nimbus together.

That opening string of adjectives describes nothing so well as a dream. Or, it would be more apt to say, the scene is being revised into a dreamscape.

As we next move back on the horizontal, we strike what Belitt calls a "vertical" distance. John Pope-Hennessy compared *The Rout of San Romano* to "a scene set before a drop curtain, in which we are perpetually conscious of an incongruity between the false space represented on the backcloth and the real space of the stage." This false space is the garden—with its harrowed fields and fertile pomegranates—that has always opposed Armageddon in Belitt's imagination. But even his bright ideal is shrouded here; the pomegranate becomes an eclipsed sun, the season a furnace awaiting its human sacrifice. The fruitful and nurturing, the sustaining maternal background, is powerless amid the terrorisms of war. Like Cain, the land is branded. And though not capitalized, the word "holocaust" reminds us we are dealing not with an incident but with a condition, both private and historical.

The third part, "Encounter," dramatically completes his description of the action portrayed. Belitt's details don't exactly tally with those of the Uffizi picture; the relationship of the contenders is reversed, not the antagonist but the horseman behind him is wearing "a turban's swathe," and so on. But then the poet is after sensation rather than accuracy. The line-lengths are cut into nervous flashes. Tension is displaced unto weapons and strategies. The archetypal couple, Contender and Antagonist, are paired off in mortal combat, like elemental forces, or any father and son. "And the contest begins." In all his work, Belitt has been drawn to such moments, to acts of destruction and transformation, of awful change.

With "A Reading of Entrails," we suddenly depart—"withdraw" is Belitt's word—from the world of the painting. As before we had retreated back to some hybrid classical landscape of sybil and haruspicator. Why? The dreamwork mingling of motifs here is as important as the sybil and her portents to indicate that we are on the borders of the unconscious, where myth and chaos meet. Poems themselves draw chance into legend, are precisely that stylization of impulses. The sybil here is a muse. Belitt summons all the random details he'd earlier heaped up, and reflexively weaves them into a "decoration by Uccello"—a tapestried poem within the poem of static, exquisite textures:

A foreground of horses:
> *turquoise and cinnamon shod*
With a jeweler's crescent; the straining albino,
His contemplative chessman's head in his bridle's rosette
Calm in the contact of riders.
> *A navy of javelins*
On the overturned horses—a carousel's
Splintered rotations.

Here is the fable, the dream, the word-painting, the pastoral battleground. From language itself springs the true garden: "The cinquefoil thicket laced with a pollen of poppies / The dismounted anonymous god in the goldleaf rubble." And nowhere is Belitt's characteristic idiom more lavishly displayed. In just the few lines I've quoted the short syllables scurry between rich assonantal occasions; the architectonic consonants mass and hold the line against the syntactical momentum.

"Il y avait chez lui non ce goût de la difficulté qu'on lui a encore une fois à tort reproché, mais un goût du risque qu'on ne peut nier. . . . Il aimait à penser que les limites qu'il dépassait lui permettaient d'avancer encore et, plutôt que de rester immobile et de se satisfaire d'une virtuosité quelconque, il préférait de nouvelles directions."—Philippe Soupault.

Such a balanced, moralizing conclusion might have satisfied another writer; but not Belitt, who in the last part, "Festival of Anger," takes the poem in new directions. They are not easy for the reader—or this reader, at any rate—to follow. The first four stanzas seem a fantasia on the idea and import of combat. A range of heroes, from classical or Arthurian mythologies, is finally concentrated to a category, and literally embodied as "Fighters in the blood." Standing against these heroes are the "horned and necessitous ones." "Old changelings

of the gorged heart of the toad" seem to be the adversarial principle of evil—
what opposes and negates. The toad, the hedgehog, the Antagonist—all are
old signs and names for the devil. However this may be, the combat is ritual-
ized, as ever-present in the self as in history, in art as in the unconscious. It is
the legend that underlies chance. What "hardens its venom" also (in lines that
ceremonially rhyme)

> breaks
> The providential fountain from the stone
> And looks like history or hope, but takes
> A moment's inadvertence for its own.

"I would fight that battle," the poet continues. He calls it "that battle after
the battle"—that is, the private or "inward" combat made manifest "outward"
in art, by a picture (woven with a shuttle, drawn with a pencil, etched with a
burin) or a poem ("The matched and extortionate word"). Belitt combines
Gilgamesh and Faust with his own oedipal struggles in one last attempt to contain the battle by defining it—"The battle of the monster and the mothers." All
along, the battle has been a psychomachia. The Uccello painting has func-
tioned, then, as a decorative screen—just as a poem may—for this primary
conflict. The neurotic pageant is various but unchanging; there is only "the
imagining / Begetter and the habitual figures of his quarrel." Having uncov-
ered this streak in himself—this "furrow blazing like a revelation"—the poem
can return, in a quiet diminuendo, to images from Uccello, both his "landscape of surrender" and the now flourishing garden beyond. As a token of his
achievement, a crowning laurel is added to the pomegranate.

The little heraldic device at the very end of the poem, echoing the conclusion of part 3, is taken from a detail in the painting. The hare is a traditional
symbol of lust, but that overtone doesn't predominate. The hare is also known
as a lunar creature, and represents feminine periodicity, rebirth, the tender
wisdoms—here pursued by the hunting greyhound, and threatened by the
"invisible thong of the snare." This chase has been run, these opponents
joined, these threats entertained and postponed, this battle pieced together in
the poems of book after book, Ben Belitt's lifetime in the art.

8 . WOMAN IN WHITE

?

?

?

?

?

?

?

?

Even during her lifetime, Emily Dickinson had become a legend. To Amherst townfolk and to a small literary community beyond, she was the famously eccentric recluse, a sweet spinster genius cracked with moonlight, a white witch who let gingerbread down on a string from her bedroom window for the neighborhood children. After her death, early (partial and "corrected") editions of her poems fashioned a new legend, of the delicate curiosity whose "bolts of melody" were stitched like a homemade sampler. It was not until 1955, seventy years after her death, that an accurate and comprehensive edition of Dickinson's poems appeared; a popular reading edition followed in 1961, a proper biography in 1974. Only in the short decades since has her true power at last, and almost abruptly, been revealed. The Dickinson myth—again adjusted, this time to her position as one of the language's great poets—has become an industry. She has been made over into an example of nearly every critical fashion; her story has been rewritten to include melodramas from abortions to lesbian affairs, and her role in the culture been changed—now antiwar crusader, now feminist pioneer. Each time, she slips free, of biographical absurdities as of any other reductive classification. Her life remains a puzzle, at once demurely conventional and powerfully estranged. And her poems remain a mystery, plain as a daisy and as cryptic as any heart.

Emily Dickinson was born on December 10, 1830, in the large brick Federal house her grandfather had built, three blocks from the Amherst town green. She lived her life and died in this house. It was called "The Homestead," and she once described it as her unfallen world: "Home is a holy thing," she wrote to her brother, "nothing of doubt or distrust can enter its blessed portals. I feel it more and more as the great world goes on and one and another forsake, in whom you place your trust—here seems indeed to be a bit of Eden which not the sin of *any* can destroy." A middle child, she was close to her older brother Austin and younger sister Lavinia; all three were dominated by their father Edward, the remote dour puritanical God of her Eden. "His heart was pure and terrible," she wrote after his death. Dickinson's mother, after whom the poet was named, was a meek, unhappy, resigned woman. Only when Dickinson finally became her mother's mother—nursing her through a long final illness—did the daughter feel any sympathy for her. In truth, she was alone, and her earthly paradise was language. "My Lexicon—was my only companion," she later wrote.

"My Mother does not care for thought," one of her letters recalls, "—and Father, too busy with his Briefs—to notice what we do—He buys me many Books—but begs me not to read them—because he fears they joggle the Mind. They are religious—except me—and address an Eclipse, every morning—whom they call their 'Father.' " Though delicate health forced her to withdraw after only a year at the Mount Holyoke Female Seminary, she had received there, as earlier at the Amherst Academy, an excellent education— rigorous studies in mathematics, geography, and the sciences, in music and philosophy, languages, rhetoric, and logic. But before all else came religion. Amherst, though a college town, was a staunchly Puritan community. The air everywhere rang with themes of death and salvation; ordinary events were emblems of great states of soul, the world merely the text to be deciphered for God's intentions. Religious revivals periodically swept the town. As a young woman, Dickinson both yearned for and resisted the sometimes harrowing call to conversion. "Christ is calling everyone here," she wrote to a friend in 1850, "All my companions have answered. . . . I am standing alone in rebellion, and growing very careless." At Mount Holyoke she was put with the no-hopers, determined to preserve her identity and cultivate her intelligence. "The shore is safer," she wrote at twenty to her friend Abiah Root, "but I love to buffet the sea—I can count the bitter wrecks here in these pleasant waters, and hear the murmuring winds, but oh, I love the danger!"

She read the books in her father's library, cultivated a series of passionate, anxious friendships, and watched as her friends married or died young. "Parting is all we know of heaven," her famously bleak lines have it, "And all we need of hell." Abandoned to a daughter's duty, but choosing the terms of a seclusion necessary to her genius, she gradually retired into a homebound world of words. "Because I could not say it," she wrote in a letter, "I fixed it in the Verse." Words became her source of empowerment, her sense of self, her means to wrestle with the demons of faith or the seraphic exultations of solitude, her way both to preserve and parse her perceptions. "Sometimes I write one," she once said of words, "and look at his outlines till he glows as no sapphire." But from the start, she realized the gem has a cutting edge, that she could use "words like Blades . . . / And every One unbared a Nerve / Or wantoned with a Bone." Gem and blade both resolve to that *certain slant of Light* her poems cast, and by means of which she discovered for herself a vocation higher than any calling, an inspiration or poetic "breath" that entitled her to eternity:

For this—accepted Breath—
Through it—compete with Death—
The fellow cannot touch this Crown—
By it—my title take—
Ah, what a royal sake
To my necessity—stooped down!

Precisely when and why she began writing poems is as impossible to say about Dickinson as about any poet. By the late 1850s she was copying out her poems and binding them into packets—four or five sheets of folded and threaded writing paper. Nearly fifty of these booklets were discovered in her bedroom bureau after her death. Of the 1,775 poems of hers we have today, only eleven were published in her lifetime, all of them anonymously. During the last two decades of her life, she wrote little. The floodtide was 1862–1863, when hundreds of poems, and many of her greatest, were written. Some critics suggest a nervous crisis; others a surge in confidence. It was just at this time, in fact, aware of her power but uncertain of her possibilities, that she turned to someone for help. Encouraged by a sympathetic essay, "Letter to a Young

Contributor," she read in the *Atlantic Monthly* in April 1862, Dickinson sent its author, the critic Thomas Wentworth Higginson, four poems and a letter asking him to say "if my Verse is alive." His reply was respectful, but he judged the poems "not for publication." She wrote back to thank him "for the surgery—it was not so painful as I supposed," and enclosed three more poems. When Higginson again wavered—finding the poems "remarkable, though odd"—her reaction had a proud, sardonic edge to its submission:

> I smile when you suggest that I delay "to publish"—that being foreign to my thought, as Firmament to Fin—
> If fame belonged to me, I could not escape her—if she did not, the longest day would pass me on the chase—and the approbation of my Dog, would forsake me—then—My Barefoot-Rank is better—
> You think my gait "spasmodic"—I am in danger—Sir—
> You think me "uncontrolled"—I have no Tribunal.

Her fourth letter to him, a month later, is bolder in its declaration of her ambition: "Perhaps you smile at me. I could not stop for that—My Business is Circumference—An Ignorance, not of Customs, but if caught with the Dawn—or the Sunset see me—Myself the only Kangaroo among the Beauty."

"The only sin is limitation," Emerson wrote in his essay "Circles." "The life of man is a self-evolving circle, which, from a ring imperceptibly small, rushes on all sides outward to new and larger circles, and that without end. . . . Step by step we scale this mysterious ladder; the steps are actions, the new prospect is power." When Dickinson boasts her business is circumference, she locates her ambition on the edge of things, a God's-eye view onto the new prospects. "The Bible dealt with the Centre, not with Circumference," she wrote in a late letter, and all along she meant both to subvert and to transcend the orthodox. Her business can mean that, like Whitman, she contains multitudes—contradictory states of feeling and paradoxical ideas. It also means she writes as the solitary outsider, looking back at worldly life and outward to cosmic matters; she sometimes even portrays herself as a monster, an outcast. But her business with circumference, above all, means she is concerned to *define*, to take the measure of extremes, of gain and loss, of what she calls Anguish and Bliss.

"Something in the sight / Adjusts itself to Midnight," one poem avows. God's withdrawal from the land—"so huge, so helpless to conceive"—is an abiding theme:

Much Gesture, from the Pulpit—
Strong Hallelujahs roll—
Narcotics cannot still the Tooth
That nibbles at the soul.

Loathe to doubt the principle of God's existence, she is at the same time eager
to undermine complacent or oppressive myths about our Father and his
"House of Supposition." And though she writes with a naturalist's eye about
the New England landscape—the apple bough beyond the window, the bee at
his flowery task, the sowing of days and harvest of seasons—she treats Nature
as she does Divinity, as an emblem of the self. "Gethsemene— / Is but a
Province—in the Being's Centre—," and "the Angle of a Landscape" may
reveal only "a newer Wilderness / My Wilderness has made." What her poems
regard continually, and with a restless moral scrutiny, is the soul's abyss, the
experience of human isolation, the threatened, vulnerable self "homeless at
home" in this world.

She is skeptical of appearances, enraptured by ideas, contemptuous of judgment. Her tone—sometimes within a single stanza—can veer sharply from the
playful to the haunted, from the surreal to the epigrammatic. Meanings slide.
Traditional themes and prosody are set askew. Her irregular lines, elliptical
syntax, slant rhymes, and enigmatic metaphors may sometimes distract a
reader from hearing that most often her poems are written in common measure, the metrical format for ballads, hymns, and nursery rhymes. In much the
same way, she takes the traditional language of belief—terms like *Immortality*
and *Salvation, Eternity* and the *Argument from Design*—and empties them of
any reassurance, then charges them anew with a startling force.

When Higginson—who she once said "saved my Life" by his interest in her
work—asked her for a photograph of herself, Dickinson demurred, and
described herself as "small, like the Wren, and my Hair is bold, like the
Chestnut Bur—and my eyes, like the Sherry in the Glass, that the Guest
leaves." The woman's self-effacement disguised the poet's bold strategies. She
stayed in her room, dressed in white, like a page on which the universe would
inscibe its secrets. At her funeral, Higginson looked at her, in her white dress,
in a white casket, and marvelled that she had "not a gray hair or wrinkle, & perfect peace on the beautiful brow." But when he had first visited her years earlier, he wrote of her "excess of tension . . . She was much too enigmatical a

being for me to solve in an hour's interview." "I was never with any one," he wrote to his wife, "who drained my nerve power so much. Without touching her, she drew from me." His experience in the Amherst parlor was the same as any reader's today. She draws from us the very terms of our selfhood. She draws us on toward "the Glimmering Frontier that skirts the Acres of Perhaps."

9. Wildness Asking for Ceremony

?

?

?

?

?

?

?

?

?

"On Monday," Delmore Schwartz wrote, "I sent some of your poems, hurriedly and perhaps poorly chosen, to Laughlin." Schwartz's letter to Jean Garrigue, dated August 1, 1942, was meant to encourage her. As teacher and student, they had met that summer at the Cummington School of the Arts, and Garrigue had been depressed. Marianne Moore, with whom Garrigue also worked that summer in the Berkshires, noticed the young poet's uncertainties and discontents, and by praising the well-knit vigilance and experienced tone of her work Moore may have been indirectly urging Garrigue to cultivate those same qualities in her life. Part of Garrigue's self-doubts were temperamental, and shadowed her whole career. Part were any beginner's wooziness in the face of daunting traditions and possibilities. Over the years Garrigue managed to dispel those doubts, most often by making them into art. Her confidence—what Robert Lowell once called her "big sweep and untiring deftness"—cost. But over and over she found new ways to control her experience and refresh her art. Ten years after their first meeting, Moore was astonished by the power of Garrigue's poems, and by the capacity of her feelings both to resist and accept. Twenty years later, another phrase of Moore's, from one of her last letters to Garrigue, remains the best description of the resolve, the drama, the achievement of Garrigue's work. You've shown, wrote Moore, an "unexampled heroism."

But none of this was evident at the start. "I know that you are a good poet," Schwartz's letter continues, "and perhaps to be a very good one and this makes me think, How sad that you should waste time and emotion on self-doubt. How might you be persuaded that I mean and perhaps know what I say about the goodness of your poems?" To become A Very Good Poet had been Garrigue's lifelong ambition. When they were young, her sister asked her what she most wanted in life. "Fame as a writer," she answered. Her sister has also recalled Garrigue as "an impatient and fretful little child," only soothed by music; as a rebellious student, expelled from school for bad behavior, but spending hours in her third-floor room at home reading Shelley, Keats, Swinburne, the Imagists, and H.D. —who, she once said, "made daring to write poetry seem possible." She went to hear Edna St. Vincent Millay read, and excitedly spent all her savings—$25—on a first edition of Millay's poems.

Garrigue was born in Evansville, Indiana, on December 8, 1912 (though the date she gave later was 1914). Raised in Indianapolis, and educated at the University of Chicago (where her roommate was Marguerite Young) and at Iowa, she had a Midwesterner's yearning for the cultural blandishments and social freedoms of the East. She visited Paris as soon as possible, and when she first arrived to live in New York City, she changed her name from the demure Gertrude Louise Garrigus to the more poetic Jean Garrigue. (The sexual ambiguity of her first name may be noted, and the version of her surname brings it closer to its proper French spelling, Garrigues, a Huguenot family from the Languedoc. Originally, the name was Garric, meaning "oak." The English actor David Garrick was from the same family. The French word *garrigue* means "moor" or "wasteland.") It was in New York in 1940, she later recalled, "that I felt myself delivered and as it were in possession of a tongue. All dates from that, despite a lost trunkful of the proverbial journals, notes, poems and prose—that trail of attempts and explorations the writer must blaze."

The bluntly titled *Thirty-Six Poems and a Few Songs*—Garrigue's name for her share of *Five Young American Poets*—has just thirty-six poems in the collection, so her title is meant slyly to stress the implicit lyric character of all the work. In a brief preface to her poems, Garrigue declares her devotion less to the example of the English metaphysical poets than to T. S. Eliot's widely influential version of their strengths. She praises—and thereby asks the reader to notice in her own poems—a style that jostles its quartz-sides and lengthens its perspectives with irony, that "allows gracious license to the fluctuations, recoils and most delicate expeditions into the matter of the subject." Poetic "truth" rests in relationships, and it is the poet's task both to describe and to connect. If his subject is, say, a hill, then "he wants all of the hill that is useful, that is, to his poem: its roughness or its glabrous surface, its rocks or peaked loaf, its nubile or spartan look: but he also wants to interpret, that is, to humanize, to bring it into the realm of his, the poet's, into conjunction with railroad ties or sunflowers, lighthouses or Love or God." These early poems by Garrigue, with their pulsing rhythms, lightly brushed-in rhymes, and elaborately worked conceits, are very much in the high style of the day—that day being the time of the New Critics, who insisted that a poem represented an action, that its dramatic effects were extensions of its voice, that it unfolded its meanings not with any discursive logic but in an expressive complex of images. Poems of this period most nearly resembled the creative mind itself: sedulous, self-reflective, allusively cultured, with an aloof integrity and an evident, though not necessarily apparent, continuity between their manifold surfaces and their unconscious depths or motives. From the start, though, Garrigue's voice sounded strange. She tried for a "poetic diction" that could speak of feelings glimpsed beneath her thought-provoking designs, that could explore "our landscape of love . . . [a] rich and violent country." Romantic and symbolist motifs—moon and mirror, dark wood and golden hair—abound. But the lapidary eloquence of her textures wants continually to give way. Underneath the brook's face is, skull-like, "a building made by shadow." Beyond the restraining glassen surfaces is "the improvident flood." It is this tension that gives her poems their force, their compelling restlessness.

> Leaping and leaping our hearts,
> Sight staggered; if landscape was
> Different than we, so were we,
> So were we, falling, ourselves from
> Ourselves cut off, emblem of love
> Torn in two.

When he was in prep school, John Ashbery now recalls, he read these first poems by Garrigue with a thrilled eagerness. There was "a surreal, dream-like quality" to them he later found only in French poetry, and "a strangeness that I sympathized with." Both *The Ego and the Centaur* (1947) and *The Monument Rose* (1953) continue the baroque anxieties, the extravagant rhetorical gestures, the estranging sympathies of her first book. The poems are divinations and spells. States of being are conjured. Language is translated into experience. To be sure, one hears occasional echoes in that language. Here is Auden (while at Cummington, Garrigue had appeared in a production of *The Ascent of F-6*):

> The time for thinking is useless,
> The time for acting is done;
> It seems in this noisy city
> Girded by tracks and by rivers
> Not even the sky is natural
> With its supple, escaping clouds.

And here Eliot:

> In the garden the roses scattered
> When under the wickets I came
> To their blooming there on the mound.

This could be Hart Crane or Dylan Thomas:

> O nuptial drug and condiment of rite,
> O tempter to an inwardness of sight,
> Dwarfs, indigo, within whose opera,
> O bridal jest, you circummortal us,
> Nuptial of vacancy who wizards us.

Garrigue had first read Dylan Thomas in *Poetry* in 1938, and been struck by "the shock and dazzle and extraordinary newness of his language, concept and organization. . . . He skirts meaning, walks around it and above it." In his turn, Thomas later called her "a deeply serious poet with a fine ear and a lovely, dangerous voice of her own." In her first three books, Garrigue conceived her own ambition, her own *voice*, in a manner not unlike Thomas's. She cared not for the beat of the line but for the cadence of the sentence, charged with emotion. She wanted what Coleridge called "the figured language of thought," a rapturous cascade of metaphor, and a transfiguring moral energy. Above all she wanted a new language for poetry: explosive, spellbound, profusive. But the language is to be both scrim and scalpel; she is continually impatient to push words past their easy referential duties, to use language not to recount but to create experience. Among her papers, she left this undated note:

> It is the poet's faith that there is a reality, if not realities upon realities back of, behind, beyond the enchanting surfaces and appearances of "reality." Perhaps his most strenuous occupation is to peel himself, to divest himself, to bare himself of the evil enchantments that "surface reality" man cast upon him in order that he may strip himself down to that level of seeing and feeling whereby his reality may be able to meet the reality within and behind what is seen and known to the senses.

In the 1950s, Garrigue began to teach. First at Bard, later at Queens, the New School, the University of Connecticut, and at Smith, she taught poetry courses. One of her students at Bard, the poet Grace Schulman, remembers her "affection for and devotion to her students—not a hovering maternal affection but a deep respect for their vocation and their hopes." It was during this period too that her poems entered a new phase—one, ironically, less studied than her early work. Her ambition had matured, and the poems, if less intense, are more poised and complex. "A Figure for J. V. Meer," at once a homage to Vermeer and an emblematic self-portrait, views the objects in the world, the *given*, as "Signs for the ungiven thing / She converses with on that light gathering in." In Vermeer's paintings, the glistening seed pearls scattered everywhere are meant by the artist both to reflect light and to create it within the picture's frame. So too Garrigue's heightened rhetorical deployment of details. Each rose or blood drop is an atomy of passion, each a translucence "Like a clarity of being become / A concordance, an equation, this light / With the soul transformed in its chamber." A clarity that both balances and transforms is the hallmark of Garrigue's middle period.

Each book now is anchored by a long poem: "For the Fountains and Fountaineeers of Villa d'Este," "Pays Perdu," "The Grand Canyon," "Studies for an Actress." She once said, "I prefer elaborate structures to functional slick ones. Chopin, Keats, and Proust were early powerful influences. So were mountains and water." For her, art is as "real" as nature, Proust as natural as a mountain, as elemental as water. Art, in fact, is a magical way for her to enter into the natural world. To gaze at the fountains of the Villa d'Este long enough to see through their exquisite artificiality is to become transfigured, to return to a natural state in a manner entirely mythological:

> I am dense as lichen,
> Primordial as fern,
> Or, like that tree split at its base,
> Covert for winter creatures and water-retreated life,
> Tip with my boughs very serpent green,
> Or in a grand spirit of play
> Spurt water out of my nostrils.

A gloss on this poem's "elaborate structure," and on her aesthetic in general, may properly be found in her essay on Chartres. To enter this or the other long Garrigue poems is like her own impression of entering the great Gothic cathedral: "the length and the height, the confined vastity, the determined obscurity clarified by windows of burning light." To contemplate the whole is to wonder "by what vigorous rationalism and dense pounds of masonry an interior all spirit is kept contained."

"Pays Perdu" is a ramble, a diaristic account that draws on Garrigue's strengths as a novelist. Set in Keats's imagined Provence, the poem is itself a landscape, with stretches of verse interspersed with heaped-up prose. Relaxed and intimate, its tone and control are a measure of the authority of Garrigue's style in these middle years. Her favorite subjects are travel (almost always a voyage inward as well) and love (usually toured as a foreign place). Love—bad love, wronged love, futile or wrecked love—was her counterpart to imagination. What she lost in life—in a passionate life, fraught with affairs with both sexes, with abortions and obsessions—she tried to recover in art. If, as one poem has it, art is a cracked looking glass, it shows us the "Grand ceremonials of a play / By which we tried to live a passion out / By every nuance in a little room." That little room is, finally, the stanza of a poem. And that mirror—image of the widened eye opposite, and of the cloud-crossed moon outside—is, like the poem, a witchery held up to see one's secret life in, and "though the smoke is gone there is some fire / In saying so."

"The Grand Canyon" has been singled out by some critics as Garrigue's finest poem. Certainly it is her most virtuosic. There are just four sentences, but one of them swirls through 109 lines. That sentence begins with the phrase

"I am lonely," and then fills up with an astonishing plenitude of descriptive and speculative detail. *Facts, things*—cliffs and roots and wedges of shadow—inhibit her confrontation with the Sublime, which is the poem's true subject. Garrigue was teaching on the West Coast in 1971, and fell seriously ill. She was diagnosed with Hodgkin's disease, and decided to return east for treatment. She had just a year left to live (she died on December 27, 1972), and it was on that slow, anxious cross-country trip that she stopped to visit the Grand Canyon. With those facts in mind, as they are not in the poem, it is hard not to scrutinize the scene differently. In the very first stanza, for instance, there is an ordinary observation that turns menacing: "the raven that flies, scouting above it, / of the hooked face and the almost flat sleek wings." Then notice how the foreboding seeps into the next lines:

> I am lonely,
> knocked out, stunned-sleepy,
> knocked out by the terraced massed faces
> of the brute Sublime,
> color inflamed,
> when I came to the edge and looked over:
> violaceous, vermillion
> great frontal reefs, buttes,
> cliffs of rufous and ocher angles,
> promontories, projections, jutments, outjuttings
> and gnarled mirlitons, so it seemed,
> twisting up out of depth beyond depth
> gnarled like the juniper tree
> rachitic with wind I hung on to
> as the raven's wing, glassy in the light of its black,
> slid over me . . . .

"This maw, gash / deepest in the world," then, is death itself—Emptiness and Nothing, at once infernal and alluring. Perhaps to defend herself against the merely personal in this poem, Garrigue structures the episode in wholly lyric terms. This is not a woman confronting her own mortality, though that is a powerful and troubling undercurrent; instead, she has devised an altogether grander, nearly mythological encounter. It is a poem about what she calls "threshholds." Faced with a "stillness / stinging, overpowering the ear, / pure condition of the original echoing soundlessness," she steps into words, steps up to the poet's task: naming, describing, praising in an ecstatic burst of language.

Though it may be her best poem, "The Grand Canyon" is not finally a characteristic one, just as the lyric is not in the end her truest voice. "Studies for an Actress," a sort of refracted self-portrait, veers through thoughts, through baffling powers she would appease and cannot, through unsatisfied memories and emblematic longings. The pageant of dreamwork, the puzzle of the will as it rushes at love, those mysterious ways by which the self is assembled and sustained—Garrigue threads her way through these mazes with a series of questions, testing each step, and in the end surrendering to the very process itself:

> She prays if nothing else to be
> In some dissolving medium of light,
> A pond that's set to catch the arrowy beams,
> Reflective and obedient as that.
> She prays then to change
> If it's in changing that things find repose.
> She prays to praise. She prays to be
> Condensed now to one desire
> As if it were very life performing her.

"The dialogue of self with soul, the quarrel of self with world" is how she once described her work, and she wanted a language "which takes its rhythms from heartbeat and blood." Only to be intrigued by the sumptuary textures of Garrigue's verse is to risk missing the sharply dramatic nature of her poems. It was not Marianne Moore to whom Garrigue looked as a model (though she wrote a critical study of Moore), but Emily Dickinson. She admired Moore, but identified with Dickinson. In an essay about Dickinson that clearly projects the impulses of her own imagination, Garrigue links her with Donne and the other metaphysicals who "had fed on awe."

> The unattainable was her passion and her woe, her ecstatic bereavement, that loss she gets strange gain from. That restless mind, driven to an extremity and, visited by velocities of intuition, a kind of victim of its own phosphorescent gleanings from the seas of the dimensions she perished but survived in. Is she not odd, oblique, quivering, overstrung, "blue-peninsulaed"? . . . No substances were common for her. She saw them all

as rare. Her effort was to achieve the language that would allow their rareness to be known. . . . Dramatic rather than lyrical, she is direct, vigorous, and so original that she suffered for it throughout her lifetime.

Dickinson's langauge she hears as dissonant, compressed, angular, introspective yet suited for conflict, above all flamboyantly emotional.

In Garrigue's view, love, death, and poetry for Dickinson were parts of a trinity that meet at the "junction of Eternity." Yet Garrigue's own last collection, though it triangulates these abiding themes, is also her most engaged and timely work. *Studies for an Actress*, published posthumously in 1973, marks the third stage or full maturity of her art. There are elegies and love letters, but also political meditations. It is true that her early books included poems like "That Fascist Bird" and "V-J Day," but politics are their occasion, not their subject. Her late poems, on the other hand, although they cast a cold eye on "our swollen pigsfoot of a state," are never merely polemical. As Adrienne Rich once observed about them, Garrigue "evokes a sense of contemporary helplessness, not merely before shattering public events, but individual reticence and disrelation." The most important relationship in Garrigue's life was her long and troubled liaison with the radical novelist Josephine Herbst, who died in 1969. It may have been Herbst who awakened Garrigue's political conscience. "You would have it that we may break out of ourselves," Garrigue wrote in her elegy for Herbst, "The solitude breaking down also." But the times themselves—the late sixties—were volatile, and Garrigue was a thinking woman. History had raided her dreameries. In the face of "friends retreating into wordlessness . . . Like love going back on what it'd said and sworn," she feels impelled to defend clarity against deceit, to confront "the crooked coldness, emptiness / That slacks the purpose in a waste of war," to bear witness to "the pain of others beginning to show through." Her outraged moral conscience—as she dramatizes it in "Resistance Meeting: Boston Common"—is finally an extension of her threatened sense of self, her vulnerable sense of romantic poethood:

An order that has always been known,
known, forgotten, denied
under the pressure not to distinguish what is true from what is necessary,
flying the flag of expediency,
which is the mere power of the mind
or the idea, the pure idea of man

witness on his own terms to what he knows,
making and re-making what he is.

For all its poise and precision, its new commitments and curiosities, *Studies for an Actress* remains a charged example of what Jane Mayhall once rightly called Garrigue's "reckless grandeur." The book's serenity is counterbalanced by a "myth-making mist and resurrecting light." Hoping to make the glitter break into song in her late poem "Moondial," she reminds us "we are animals of the moon." By its light, we are permitted flashing glimpses of both the chaos and the order at the heart of things. Here are trees, dressed in moonlight:

Perfect they stood and were the more perfected.
We thanked the light for falling as it did
To show their every tangle in the whole
Of wildest, most cross-flowing intricacy.
Such wildness asked for ceremony.

A wildness that evokes ceremony goes to the heart of Jean Garrigue's imagination. "I like comets, lightning, fireworks," she once confessed, and might as well have been describing her preference for Wyatt, Donne, Marvell, Hopkins, Yeats, Hart Crane, and Dylan Thomas. It was by flashes of lightning that she wrote, the true Romantic poet of her generation. "My salvation," she confided to her notebook, "is in moments; by actions of perception and redemption." Her notebooks are filled with such self-revealing sketches: "Still kept from the feast I tremble before the crumb that falls and my hunger makes that a feast." *The moment, the flash, the crumb*—these are what she takes up into her great hunger. "Where to begin the poem," she asks. "As close as you can to the nerve." *Hunger, nerve, grandeur*—these are what she gives back. At the end of her life, in her great poem of departure, "Grief Was to Go Out, Away," she is alone on a beach, and like Whitman or Elizabeth Bishop in similar poems she broods over what she must abandon:

Grief was just in the having
Of so much heart pulse gone out and away
Into absence and the spent shadow
Of what ran from our fingers as ripples
Of shadow over the sand and what eluded
In a bending of mirrors the tipped tints and reflections

And was just so much running down the packed sands'
Mile-wide blondness of bird-tracked floor.

The enormity of the ambition, the splendor of the achievement—both make
more poignant still one simple entry in her notebook, where the poet looks back
on her own career: "I lived for certain grandeurs that fade fast—me, JG."

10 . AT HER OTHER DESK

?

?

?

?

?

?

?

?

?

?

In the years since her death, Elizabeth Bishop has triumphed. Neither the tides of literary fashion nor the sort of feminist boosterism she herself deplored account for this phenomenon. It's simply that more and more readers have discovered the enduring power of her work—quicksilver poems that are lined with dark moral clouds. A couple of decades ago, it seemed her beefier contemporaries—Robert Lowell, John Berryman, Theodore Roethke, or Randall Jarrell—would tip history's scales. But her fastidious rigor has lasted better than their more sprawling, hit-or-miss ambitions. No one ever accused them of being "perfect" poets. But that has been the password to any discussion of Bishop's work. "Perfection" is a two-edged compliment. In Bishop's case it can refer both to the exquisitely controlled textures and mirrory depths of her work and to the fact that her reputation—like that of her first mentor, Marianne Moore—is based on a very slim output.

As a young woman she vowed "never to publish anything until I thought I'd done my best with it, no matter how many years it took—or never to publish at all." In fact, during her lifetime she published (apart from a few stories and essays) just ninety poems, in books that appeared only once a decade. That each poem is an astonishment, masterly in its command of tone and detail, only left her readers eager for more. With the publication in 1994 of *One Art*, a handsome selection of letters, her work abruptly quadrupled in bulk. As her friend Robert Lowell once predicted, "When Elizabeth Bishop's letters are published (as they will be), she will be recognized as not only one of the best, but one of the most prolific writers of our century."

What do we expect from a poet's letters? Keats, with his spontaneous brilliance, set an ideal standard few other poets have matched. Byron, Dickinson — their letters are themselves literature. But the lion's share of correspondence by modern poets that has so far appeared — Frost, say, or Yeats or Stevens — is usually of interest merely to scholars. Still, readers pore over letters looking for clues. We expect letters to be a sort of cold frame for poems. And, wanting to take a human measure of someone we know intimately but abstractly through poems, we expect a less varnished view of the writer's true personality, something altogether more complex than a distilled poetic "voice." *One Art* satisfies both expectations.

One letter here, written to Marianne Moore in 1946, in part describes a bus trip in Nova Scotia: "Early the next morning, just as it was getting light, the driver had to stop suddenly for a big cow moose who was wandering down the road. She walked away very slowly into the woods, looking at us over her shoulder. The driver said that one foggy night he had to stop while a huge bull moose came right up and smelled the engine. 'Very curious beasts,' he said." Readers of Bishop will recognize that episode as the basis for her famous poem, "The Moose," which she started writing ten years later and finally published twenty-six years later. Letters have that way — Bishop's do — of capturing seedling moments that may eventually be transplanted into moral containers and moved to the imagination's forcing house.

The self-portrait Bishop paints in these letters is of a woman more beguiling, thoughtful, melancholy, quizzical, solicitous, shy, determined, and cheerful than the woman who emerges from recent biographical studies of Bishop. She's as likely to be reading Kierkegaard as fishing for amberjack or baking a cake. But art always took the back seat to life. In letters to Marianne Moore, alongside the technical talk of diction or rhythm, there are marvelous descriptions, long and bemused, of pink salamanders or the neighbor's collie or a Vietnamese princess she'd met yesterday.

The most revealing series of letters, over many years, are to Anny Baumann, a physician who had emigrated from Germany and was a general practitioner on the staff at Lenox Hill Hospital in New York. At first she was Bishop's doctor, and later her friend and confidante. There are some friends in whom we confide, and others to whom we confess. From 1947 until her death, Bishop wrote to Dr. Baumann harrowing accounts of her struggles with asthma and alcohol, looking as much for medical advice as for emotional stability. It was to Baumann, too, that she wrote most directly of her love for Lota de Macedo Soares, the Brazilian architect with whom Bishop lived from 1951 until Lota's suicide in 1967. Lota seems to have been both mannish and maternal, sophisticated and volatile. Their years together gave Bishop the home she never had, the passionate companionship she had searched for. The stress of her work, failing health, and perhaps cracks in their relationship finally drove Lota to kill herself. One winces to read Bishop's desolated letters to Dr. Baumann during this period—letters all the more painful to read because we realize how unused she was to writing so nakedly of her emotions.

I dislike cheap psychologizing as much as Bishop did, but it is hard not to think that her being an orphan didn't influence the way she wrote letters, at least at the start. In Marianne Moore and Anny Baumann she was looking for the good parent, a figure at once severe and sympathetic, indulgent and enabling. With others as well, but particularly with Moore, Bishop writes to amuse and please, warily calculating what she thinks the other wants to hear. Her letters to Moore are laced with praise and gratitude, along with reiterated vows to "try to work and study much more seriously and thoroughly than I ever have before." Her insecurities were lifelong. Even at age fifty-three, when writing to Baumann about her decision to accept a teaching post, she pleads that Baumann "forgive me for bothering you with my vague schemes—but at the same time I hope you will approve of them!"

A line in one of Marianne Moore's poems—"the world's an orphan's home"—may also help account for the extent of Bishop's travels, and for her instinct not only to survey the exotic but to domesticate it. It is, above all, her fifteen years in Brazil that are the heart and the joy of this book. The life she established with Lota in Petropolis, along with their toucan and cats and countless household dependents, was a sort of extended family and a source of endless concern: "The sewing girl is blue and has to be cheered up; give her the radio and close the door. Then the maid cries, big hot tears, because the horrible TV we keep for her is malfunctioning and makes everyone look like dwarfs, with faces four feet long. Her second cousin, large and black, who works for Lota in the park but cut his hand badly, seem to be living with us these days and decides he'll 'help' by washing the terrace with floods of water that come to the door of my study. His wife, from whom he's separated, arrives by mistake, has an attack of asthma, gets treated, then has mild hysterics and needs a sedative. Then I have to read them the plans for the Carnival from the afternoon papers because only the man, Leonico, can read (but not too well)." How was there ever time to write?

Her years with Lota were the happiest time of her life: "I like it so much that I keep thinking I have died and gone to heaven, completely undeservedly." "It is a country," she said of Brazil, "where one feels closer to real old-fashioned life, somehow. Tragedies still happen, people's lives have dramatic ups & downs and fairy-tale endings—or beginnings." The corrupt politics and distressing underlife of Rio—"that poor shabby spoiled city"—she writes about with increasing despair. But the landscape and simple people enchanted her, and she is continually plucking a correspondent's sleeve to notice the snails big as bread-and-butter plates, or the hummingbird she has to chase out of her pantry with an umbrella, or the baptism of the bricklayer's son: so much unmenacing strangeness. "The dying out of local cultures seems to me one of the most tragic things in this century," she laments. Like her poems, her letters seem to be arranged like display cases filled with so much vanished life.

"Of course I am hopelessly old-fashioned," Bishop says of herself as well. That meant she liked to hear gossip but didn't, unfortunately, pass it on in letters. It meant, too, that her temperamental modesty and good manners lend her correspondence an admirable but sometimes frustrating reserve. The distance at which she lived from her close friends prompted the abundance of her letters to them. But she guarded an emotional distance from them as well, especially when it came to matters of the heart. The most striking instance of her reticence turns up in a 1957 exchange of letters with Robert Lowell. Lowell, in a startlingly heartfelt letter to Bishop reprinted in this book, recalls a time ten years earlier when he had wanted to propose marriage to her. In the end, he didn't propose. The years passed. He remained haunted. "I do think free will is sewn into everything we do. . . . Yet the possible alternatives that life allows us are very few, often there must be none. I've never thought there was any choice for me about writing poetry. No doubt if I used my head better, ordered my life better, worked harder, etc., the poetry would have improved, and there must be many lost poems, innumerable accidents and ill-done actions. But," he continues, "asking you is *the* might-have-been for me, the one towering change, the other life that might have been had. It was that way for these nine years or so that intervened. It was deeply buried, and this spring and summer . . . it boiled to the surface." Four months go by before Bishop answers that letter with two of her own, a few days apart—long, affectionate, chatty letters that with an unspoken embarrassment never mention Lowell's declaration.

Eight months later, in another letter to Lowell, describing a trip up the Amazon with Aldous Huxley, she is describing the Indians they met and recounts a detail that almost seems an allegory of her own suppressed feelings about Lowell's passionate outburst: "They were quite naked, just a few beads; handsome, plump, behaving just like gentle children a little spoiled. They were very curious about Huxley. One who spoke a little Portuguese said he was 'homely . . . homely.' And then one, a widower, asked me to stay and marry him. This was a slightly dubious compliment; nevertheless the other ladies along were all quite jealous. But I am finishing up a long piece about it (and hope to goodness I can sell it and start building the garage) so I won't describe it any more." There are other such moments in this book when one senses her cool but slightly trembling grip on her own panic.

Her reticence, however, never inhibits her honesty. She called it "my George Washington handicap—I can't tell a lie even for art, apparently; it takes an awful effort or a sudden jolt to make me alter facts." The scrupulous observations that are the groundwork of her poems (no wonder Darwin was her "favorite hero") are everywhere apparent in these letters as well, and extend to her estimates of friends and their work. Her opinions are always just, often uncomfortably so. Of her college classmate and friend Mary McCarthy's novel *The Group*: "It's fantastic writing—good, but without one shred of imagination, something that seems almost impossible—but Mary does it." On Robert Penn Warren: "I've always been very enamored of that red hair and that blue glass eye, although I can't stand those novels with round-breasted heroines and wicked heroes—just like *Gone With the Wind* with metaphysical footnotes." On Anne Sexton: "That Anne Sexton I think has a bit too much romanticism and what I think of as the 'beautiful old silver' school of female writing, which is really boasting about how 'nice' we were. V. Woolf, E. Bowen, R. West, etc.—they are all full of it. They have to make quite sure that the reader is not going to misplace them socially, first—and that nervousness interferes constantly with what they think they'd like to say." On Dylan Thomas: "I have met few people in my life I felt such an instantaneous sympathy and pity for, and although there must have been many things wrong, disastrously wrong, Dylan made most of our contemporaries seem small and disgustingly self-seeking and cautious and hypocritical and cold."

The compiler of One Art, Robert Giroux, was Bishop's editor and close friend. His abiding affection for her and his skillful editorial hand are the book's scaffolding, from his eloquent introduction to his deft arrangement and excisions. Giroux has had a long and distinguished career in service to literature; this edition—which he probably considered a labor of love—may well prove to be his most valuable contribution. He had over 3,000 letters to choose from, and the 541 letters he includes already make for a bulky book. There undoubtedly would have been thousands more still to sort through. After Lota's suicide, one of her former lovers spitefully destroyed all her letters from Bishop. Another former lover of Bishop's, Marjorie Stevens, burned all of hers. Even so, there are omissions that puzzle me. Missing, for instance, are letters to anyone in Brazil, during or after Bishop's long residence there. And no letters to the likes of Jane Dewey, Arthur Schlesinger, Octavio Paz, Mark Strand, Alice Toklas, Ned Rorem, Meyer Schapiro, Joseph Frank, and others whom she mentions here that she has written to. Giroux has concentrated on her circle of closest friends—old classmates, her aunt, dearest unliterary friends, Dr. Baumann, and the three eminent fellow poets to whom she wrote most carefully: Marianne Moore, Robert Lowell, and James Merrill.

It seems to me, though, that writers sometimes send their most interesting letters to strangers. The intrepid tyro, the timid fan, the inquiring critic—their unexpected, "obvious" questions often elicit more pointed and revealing answers than the familiar correspondent can. Anne Stevenson, who wrote the first critical study of Bishop's work in 1966, received many letters from Bishop in answer to her dogged queries about Bishop's poems and methods. The excerpts quoted in Stevenson's book have long since been recognized as central to our understanding of Bishop, yet none of these letters is included in One Art.

"When you write my epitaph," she once told Robert Lowell, "you must say I was the loneliest person who ever lived." Part of that loneliness she cultivated, and it remains the burden of her best poems. And part of her loneliness she assuaged with the generosity of her love and friendships, with her knack of looking at things around her through both ends of the telescope. One Art does not quite substitute for an autobiography; there are too many important facts missing. Instead, it stands as a sort of golden treasury, to be gone through in one enthralled reading and then browsed in ever after. In her notebook, Bishop once wrote that the qualities she most admired in a poem were accuracy, spontaneity, and mystery. Those same qualities shine through these letters. They prefer the anecdote to the idea; there is little of the speculative brio one finds in, say, Flannery O'Connor's letters. But Bishop has something harder to achieve: an extraordinary patience. The routines of daily life have rarely seemed so fascinating, nor the great events of the day more comic, than in her accounts of them. And beneath all the enchanting detail one senses—without their ever being dwelt upon—the anxieties, the losses, the suffering. "I think we are still barbarians," she once wrote in a letter that perfectly captures the spirit of this book, "barbarians who commit a hundred indecencies and cruelties every day of our lives, as just possibly future ages may be able to see. But I think we should be gay in spite of it, sometimes even giddy—to make life endurable and to keep ourselves 'new, tender, quick.' "

?

?

?

?

?

?

?

?

?

?

Poems are sometimes set to music, but not first written to be set. Though poets routinely claim the pedigree of song for their art, from primitive ritual chant to the lilt of sophisticated metrics, they also condescend to verse specifically written to be sung. They condescend to it by calling the result not a poem but a lyric. It is as an adjective, not as a noun, that the poet wants the word *lyric* applied to his work. On the other hand, no poet's work is so intimately known or so easily recalled as are the lyrics of, say, a Cole Porter ballad. The further modern poetry retreated into the moated castle of fragmented feelings, complex ideas, and strained allusions, the more it scorned the sentiments and schemes of popular culture. Pope and Byron were thrown out with the bathwater. This may all have been a defensive reaction against the perceived excesses of Romanticism, for at the heart of light verse—its breezy cynicism—is a tender melancholy. It may turn out to have been true that the great American song lyrics in this century have, ironically, kept alive a tradition threatened by mandarin modernists. It may be, in an age when the fashion for rumpled, brawny poems, with all the overstuffed baggage of an ego trip, and a studied anguish that sets the teeth on edge as surely as any piece of chalk screeching across the blackboard, that the tradition of prosodic virtuosity found a refuge in the song lyric. In any case, I offer Stephen Sondheim as an example.

"Anyone Can Whistle" . . . Some songs seem to be parables of their creator's imagination. *Anyone can whistle* might as well be the poet's arch opinion of his collaborator the composer—or, in Stephen Sondheim's case, one talent idly accusing another. *So someone tell me / Why can't I.* It's not that Sondheim can't, of course: the song's own lilting melody itself dismisses the question. But his point turns on a further dilemma: *What's hard is simple. / What's natural comes hard.* It's not that music, what anyone can whistle (and *natural* is a musical term), is hard for him to write—though tin-eared critics have complained his shows lack tunes an audience of Anyones might begin whistling while they walk toward the lobby. (Those critics miss the point: for one who grew up on Richard Rodgers's music, hearing Sondheim's is like listening to Stravinsky after years of Rimsky-Korsakov.) But music's impulses toward clarity of structure and force of sentiment conflict with the quintessentially ironic energies of Sondheim's lyrics. Those lyrics, on the other hand—where words can dance tangos or slay dragons—are of a complexity Sondheim had simply mastered from the start. The "difficulty" lies not in concocting their cleverness but in manipulating an intractable medium. Simplicity of utterance alone is suitable for song, and, in addition, show tunes have narrative responsibilities, a psychological duty to reveal the character of the singer, and the dramatic business of opening up that part of the musical. To have seen to all that, with a breath-catching thoroughness, and still to have those words take on an independent life in a listener's imagination, not merely to have amused but to have puzzled and challenged that listener, puts this lyricist in quite another class. Sondheim is the true poet of our theater.

The best lyricists in the long tradition of American musical theater—Ira Gershwin, Lorenz Hart, Cole Porter—shared a fondness for wordplay, for elaborated conceits, for brilliant turns of phrase that Sondheim is clearly heir to. I wouldn't say that Sondheim is cleverer than those men. I'd say he is cleverer than *any* lyricist—and that includes one with whom he has, to my mind, an overlooked affinity: William Schwenk Gilbert. I've heard grumbles that Sondheim's lyrics are *too* clever, too "intellectual," which seems an odd charge, considering that a song represents precisely that moment when our feelings are brought to the pitch of thought.

But of course the wit of Sondheim's lyrics is of a very high, a very self-conscious order. It's not just the bravura patter of, say, "A Little Priest." It's not just the metrical ingenuity and cavalcade of rhymes, where variety and substitution help both to sustain and toy with our expectations. I'm thinking, too, of Sondheim's extraordinary ability to create a dramatic scene within a song. From *West Side Story's* "America" to *A Little Night Music's* "Now—Later—Soon" or "A Weekend in the Country," these extended numbers are Sondheim's coups de théâtre, their exhilarating tensions drawn from a melody's shadow side but turning finally on the exigencies of language, one phrase plucked from the implications of another. Smaller songs can likewise turn themselves inside out: the way "sell out" is modulated from an over-the-top noun into a menacing verb in "It's a Hit!" from *Merrily We Roll Along*; the way a threatening "leave you" slides into a predatory "leave me" in "Could I Leave You?" from *Follies*. Valéry once said that poetry is not speech raised to the level of music, but music drawn down to the level of speech. That is what these songs do: music becomes speech, speech that flickers and gleams within the glass lamp of form.

One advantage Sondheim has over his peers is that his first mentor was Oscar Hammerstein. If Gershwin and Hart and Porter together comprise the smart set, all snappy sophistication and innuendo, then Hammerstein's great strength was his command of metaphor and the vivid or tender details at the heart of his lyrics. So often the effect of a Sondheim verse depends not on its quick-wittedness but on a homely detail lifted from context into wrenching significance. Here is one instance—one that sounds like Millay imitating Dickinson:

Every day a little death
In the parlor, in the bed,
In the curtains, in the silver,
In the buttons, in the bread,
Every day a little sting
In the heart and in the head.
Every move and every breath,
And you hardly feel a thing,
Brings the perfect little death.

("Every Day a Little Death," *A Little Night Music*)

The plot and tone of *Pacific Overtures* are built out of a series of metaphors, indirectly finding direction—east and west—out. The delicacies of the haiku, the enigmas of court language, the flimflam of diplomats and courtesans . . . the entire show is a view back from inside the metaphor toward its subject:

It's the fragment, not the day.
It's the pebble, not the stream.
It's the ripple, not the sea
That is happening.
Not the building but the beam,
Not the garden but the stone,
Only cups of tea
And history
And someone in a tree!

("Someone in a Tree," *Pacific Overtures*)

The dark satanic mill that roars under *Sweeney Todd* is a brilliant metaphor for the engine of commodity that the show anatomizes. The forest of *Into the Woods* is both psyche and text.

It was Gerard Manley Hopkins who claimed that a poem's style should read as "the current language heightened." That's exactly the sound of Sondheim, the idiom of foreplay and daydream, of fashionable attitudes and childhood fears, of love's resentments and anger's scruples, the idiom of the lust inside our liberal principles, the rabid fears behind our pieties, your idiom and mine: the way we live now, the way we speak with each other and with ourselves. But heightened, yes.

How does a Sondheim line work? It is hard to separate technique and tone in his lines, but together they account for the high wit of his work. Sondheim commands a prosody of astonishing virtuosity. His metrical skill is such that his measures create the character of the lyric's voice and are an extension of its moral tone. Without their musical settings, most song lyrics are as lusterless as pebbles carried home from the beach. Not Sondheim's. Usually the lines are short, crisply accented, adding appositional layers of ironic commentary to the song's thematic refrain:

Someone to hold you too close,
Someone to hurt you too deep,

Someone to love you too hard,
Happily ever after.
Someone to need you too much,
Someone to read you too well,
Someone to bleed you of all
The things you don't want to tell.
That's happily ever after,
Ever, ever, ever after in hell.

("Happily Ever After," *Company/ Marry Me a Little*)

And while it's going along,
You take it for granted some love
Will wear away.
We took for granted a lot,
But still I say:
It could have kept on growing,
Instead of just kept on.
We had a good thing going,
Going,
Gone.

("Good Thing Going," *Merrily We Roll Along*)

When the phrases are stretched to sentences, and ideas more leisurely entertained, the effect can be more exquisite than biting:

Too many people muddle sex with mere desire,
And when emotion intervenes
The nets descend.
It should on no account perplex, or worse, inspire,
It's but a pleasurable means
To a measurable end.

("Liaisons," *A Little Night Music*)

This sort of skill, a verse that is pleased with itself and is endlessly entertaining, would put Sondheim in the company of poets from Praed to Ade, masters of light verse. Light verse—so different from the lite verse ladled out nowadays by tight-lipped neo-formalists—is an art that has kept itself off where it has been pushed aside by the airier, heavier ambitions of American poetry. In its time, it has been thought too elite, too marginal, too Parnassian, too perfect in its satirical miniatures of folly, merely occasional or epigrammatic. One of the best of the tribe is Samuel Hoffenstein. Let me quote one of Hoffenstein's poems to demonstrate the family resemblance to Sondheim:

> Your little hands,
> Your little feet,
> Your little mouth—
> Oh, God, how sweet!
> Your little nose,
> Your little ears,
> Your eyes, that shed
> Such little tears!
> Your little voice,
> So soft and kind;
> Your little soul,
> Your little mind!

You can imagine, though, how Sondheim would have arrived at the same twist with altogether more intricate and pungent, more sharply observed means, with fresher rhymes and a more studied enjambment.

What Sondheim shares with a Hoffenstein or a Dorothy Parker is their instinct to invoke conventions—both poetic and social—and then subvert them. This is a part of the *realism* I would cite as the hallmark of his work. It is to this point that Sondheim's intelligence and seriousness converge, and his model here might as well be Brecht or the Auden who wrote "Calypso" and "Refugee Blues" ("Stood on a plain in the falling snow; / Ten thousand soldiers marched to and fro: / Looking for you and me, my dear, looking for you and me."). The realism of Sondheim's lyrics may be either cynical or rueful. They work variations on the abiding problem of loss: the lost paradises of childhood and first love, the loosening grip of age, the losing battle between the self and the world. His ironies are aimed at the most intimate ways we betray ourselves and then live with the fact. When sex is his subject, he will look at it from those angles which drive us to it, love and loneliness, then trace each motive back to its heartfelt illusion or heartless need. Big ballads like "Losing My Mind" or "Send in the Clowns" do so in a grand manner, with grown-up ambivalence.

Their romantic music posits what the lyrics disavow. Which is why, of course, we need the music. Sondheim's poems are made of the musical precisions in his words and the moral discourse of his melodies.

Even by themselves, his lyrics work wonderfully—not because they so readily evoke their settings but because they so readily reveal us to ourselves. When we recall his songs, we think of their quicksilver lined with clouds. But we think, too, of their ebullient charm. His scrupulous technique is a wonder because it has a temperament. Only rarely has he used wit to substitute for feelings, or merely to control them. In his best work, wit *is* feeling, the feeling that tempers others, that can both astutely caress the contours of experience and then, with a sharp turn of phrase, sound its depths, that assures us suffering is not final, while warning us that joy is transient. "The size of a man's understanding," said Dr. Johnson, "might always be justly measured by his mirth." And it is Sondheim's *understanding* I want to stress, because it most aptly characterizes his mirth and his verse. There is a penetrating intelligence and clear-eyed humanity here that can accommodate and balance the absurd and solemn, the painful and frivolous. It is, finally, a laughter in the soul.

12 . SONGS OF A CURMUDGEON

?

?

?

?

?

?

?

?

?

?

?

Once, some years ago, when he was asked what he thought about the prospect of becoming poet laureate, Philip Larkin replied, "I dream about that sometimes—and wake up screaming. With any luck they'll pass me over." They didn't. The story goes that in 1984, by which time he had long been the most admired poet of his generation in England, Larkin *was* offered the laureate's post—and refused it. Perhaps by then he knew his health was precarious. (He died of throat cancer on December 2, 1985, aged sixty-three.) But the refusal was also characteristic.

Larkin seemed to have led a life of refusals. He was an unmarried university librarian in a provincial town who described himself as looking "like a balding salmon," and who was used to renting rooms at the top of a house. He shied from publicity, rarely consented to interviews or readings, cultivated his image as right-wing curmudgeon, and grew depressed at his fame. His art, too, refused both the glamorous technical innovations and myth-mongering of Modernism as well as the will to transcendence that empowered many of his peers. He preferred to write, in clipped, straightforward stanzas, about the failures and remorse of age, about stunted lives and spoiled desires. "Deprivation," he once remarked, "is for me what daffodils were for Wordsworth." But from such refusals he fashioned a rich body of work, likely to stand as the most enduring of mid-century British poetry.

His *Collected Poems*, edited by his friend and fellow poet Anthony Thwaite, appeared in 1989. That auspicious event was accompanied by some controversy. Larkin left ambivalent instructions about his unpublished work. One clause in his will asks that it be destroyed; another clause gives his executors some discretion in the matter. To the consternation of purists, one of those executors, Thwaite, fortunately decided to ignore Larkin's doubts and give us the lot. Of the book's 242 poems, 83 appeared in print for the first time in the posthumous volume. That swelled the small output considerably, and may alter an opinion of Larkin—who published just four volumes of verse, one per decade—as a skimpy miniaturist. Thwaite made other decisions that will annoy other sorts of purists. The poems are printed chronologically, but in an editorial half-measure, the early writing, from before 1946, is placed last in the book, to one side of the poet's mature poems. And Thwaite has made only a "substantial selection" from Larkin's prodigious early work. With the later work, though the original order of each book's contents is listed in an appendix, we lose here the canny force of Larkin's own arrangements, the juxtaposition of tones and themes. But to compensate, because of this edition's precise dating, we can now watch Larkin work out a problem over several adjacent poems, written within months of each other.

When the book arrived, I turned first to the "new" poems. They range from apprentice exercises of the late thirties to occasional squibs from his last years. The general impression one takes away from reading them in bulk is an increased respect for Larkin's judgment. None of these suppressed poems will detract from his reputation, but little here will add to it. There are, though, a few surprises. Among them are several marvelous poems, most of them late (the already famous "Aubade" and the haunting "Love Again" are two of them). And several unfinished poems from his notebooks, including "The Dance" from 1963–1964, a sweet-and-sour narrative in twelve eleven-line stanzas that, if completed, would have stood with the poet's best.

The earliest poems here—"pseudo-Keats babble," Larkin once called them—date from his schooldays, and their pastiche soon gives way to more serious imitations, demonstrating how thoroughly he absorbed the strongest initial influences on his imagination, Auden and Yeats. The menaced tone and vivid rhythms of Auden pulse in these lines from a 1941 poem, "Observation":

Only in books the flat and final happens,
Only in dreams we meet and interlock,
The hand impervious to nervous shock,
The future proofed against our vain suspense . . . .

Range-finding laughter, and ambush of tears,
Machine-gun practice on the heart's desires
Speak of a government of medalled fears.

And this was soon after replaced by the austere plangencies of Yeats; warnings yielded to yearnings, and it is Yeats's voice that dominates Larkin's first collection, *The North Ship* (1954). But one is also struck now by tentative, muffled versions of what we have come to recognize as Larkin's own distinctive voice. Even with its affected teenage weariness, his apprentice sonnet "Nothing significant" sounds a note we will hear clearly throughout his career: "What was the rock my gliding childhood struck, / And what bright unreal path has led me here?"

Even more startling is to discover pre-echoes. A poem from 1943, "A Stone Church Damaged by a Bomb," seems now like a practice effort for the more famous "Church Going" of 1954. In "Spring Warning," written in 1940 and published in his school magazine, the troubling onset of spring is greeted by some who, muttering they are neither simple nor great enough to *feel*, "refuse the sun that flashes from their high / Attic windows." That phrase, of course, anticipates the great poem Larkin wrote a quarter-century later, "High Windows," the title poem of his final collection. The poem is both ironic and rueful about the brave new world of easy sex the young seem joylessly to enjoy, and the poet wonders about the happiness his elders once thought he'd laid claim to just by being young. But, in the poem's eerie last stanza, his speculation drifts into a memory, an image that accuses what it laments:

Rather than words comes the thought of high windows:
The sun-comprehending glass,
And beyond it, the deep blue air, that shows
Nothing, and is nowhere, and is endless.

The stark revelation of this endless nothing that overlooks and underlies experience is strangely offset by the nearly religious hush of the rhetoric. It is not the opposition between categories of knowledge—a relentless self-scrutiny on the one hand, and the perspectives of memory and desire on the other—that animate Larkin's best poems, but the tension between them.

The small book that first brought Larkin to prominence as a poet, and established his particular reputation, was *The Less Deceived* (1955). He chose that title, he once explained in a letter, for its "sad-eyed realism." The deceptions he conjured in order to cast out were largely self-deceptions: that romantic love or good intentions can save us from "singleness." What art exalts as "the individual," Larkin reminds is only isolation. The best poems in his two major collections, *The Witsun Weddings* (1964) and *High Windows* (1974), return to this work of disenchantment. The tone of later poems is darker, often more embittered, but throughout both books he casts a cold eye on love that always promises to solve and satisfy, the "joyous shot at how things ought to be, / Long fallen wide."

> Truly, though our element is time,
> We are not suited to the long perspectives
> Open at each instant of our lives.
> They link us to our losses: worse,
> They show us what we have as it once was,
> Blindingly undiminished, just as though
> By acting differently we could have kept it so.

The pathos of Larkin's work lies in that link with his losses, in his sense of having been obscurely betrayed. "Elsewhere underwrites my existence," he writes. The lost paradise of innocence obsesses him, and his poems. Only because of the forlorn, noisy, mean clutter of our lives does this innocence seem a "solving emptiness" for which we hunger and by which we are sickened.

"Larkin's poetry is a bit too easily resigned to grimness, don't you think?" Elizabeth Bishop once wrote in a letter to Robert Lowell. It's true that his range is rather narrow, but within its confines is a beguiling variety of tones and forms. He never repeats himself to make the same point, and his poems are more readily memorized than those of most any other postwar poet. His wit can be at once mordantly satirical and unnervingly sadhearted:

Sexual intercourse began
In nineteen sixty-three
(Which was rather late for me)—
Between the end of the *Chatterly* ban
And the Beatles' first LP.

Larkin first wanted to be a novelist, and early on wrote two novels that still give wry pleasure. His poems, too, are built up from finely observed details and portraits from the nation of shopkeepers, the England of council flats and tea towels.

Thomas Hardy, England's presiding native genius and the poet from whom Larkin learned the most, said it was his melancholy satisfaction to have died before he was out of the flesh, to have taken the ghost's view of surrounding things. "To think of life as passing away is a sadness; to think of it as past is at least tolerable." Perhaps Philip Larkin viewed this world so astutely because he wrote as if from the other side. And when most of the flashier, more blustery contemporary literature has passed away, his poetry—ghostly, heartbreaking, exhilarating—will continue to haunt.

13. THE EXILE'S SONG

?

?

?

?

?

?

?

?

?

?

?

?

It would be fair to say that Seamus Heaney is now the most successful and widely read contemporary poet in English. He stands as that rare colossus who can bestride both the Atlantic and the Irish Sea. In all three literary cultures, and at a comparatively early age, he is a critical touchstone. His books are big sellers, his readings thronged, the Nobel Prize now pinned to his reputation. In Ireland, he is considered a national hero. The English, temperamentally suspicious of hype, have had to whisk him to appearances by helicopter. In America, he has been a Harvard professor.

He has succeeded in part because, while continuing to please his admirers, he has always flown the nets of their expectations. Those Irish readers whose ambition it was that he take the place of Yeats have been disappointed by what Heaney himself has characterized as his "timid circumspect involvement" with the continuing Irish troubles, by his disavowal of any grandiloquent encounter with conscience in favor of the "sensings, mountings from the hidden places," the roots and graftings rather than the great chestnut bole. Those seeking a new Patrick Kavanagh have been disconcerted by Heaney's self-con-

(1 1 9)

scious suavities and by his persistent concern for the private life of memory, the erotics of domesticity.

Americans have always welcomed an Irish bard on stage, but this one doesn't preen or croon. Like Frost, he has charged the traditional verse line with new, buoyant tasks, but prefers not to pursue the psychology of character beyond an astute, sympathetic moralism. Like Lowell, he has perfected a wholly personal idiom and turned his own past into a general history, but he has little of Lowell's metaphysical compression or far-ranging curiosity. To be sure, he appeals to those readers tired of the garrulous weightlessness of so much recent American poetry, formless and woolly.

Still, he sometimes seems an odd alternative here, more delicate and oblique than any American counterpart. If he has abided by Valéry's warning that profundity is a hundred times easier to get than precision, and made his poems exact with Irish terms and rural lore, to American ears he remains an exotic. He is essentially a *local* poet, for whom (in his own formulation) "place symbolizes a personal drama before it epitomizes a communal situation." This doesn't always travel well; the resonance of certain words, key events, the whole geography of an Irish imagination is hard to appreciate fully.

Heaney has eluded the claims and ambitions others have set for him by being always "in between." This is his own term for a series of accidents— having been born a Catholic in the North, then settling as a northerner in the South, and always being an Irish poet in an English culture. From the start, he's been poised between the bog and the manor—that is, between the half-lit romantic heritage of a wrecked Irish language and culture and the imposing heritage of English lyric poetry. And his task has been to ruffle the lyric's decorum. He has wanted to "make it eat stuff that it has never eaten before . . . like all the messy, and it would seem, incomprehensible obsessions in the North," and to give it a new accent, disrupt its complacent graces. His early books certainly announced a "guttural muse," a gruffly lilting music drawn into clipped stanzas from a rich peat-packed word hoard. And with *North* (1975), he found his analogous way to write of the brutality and enduring anguish, "the tribal, intimate revenge" exacted by life in Northern Ireland.

The aim of his art, and the true achievement of his style, though, is not discord but balance, the sometimes estranging harmonics of conflicting demands and bequests. When, in the fine essays collected in *Preoccupations* (1980), Heaney writes about this balancing act, time and again, he describes it in terms of masculine and feminine modes of imagination—forging and incubation. The differences are embedded in language and in consciousness itself: "I think of the personal and Irish pieties as vowels, and the literary awareness nourished on English as consonants." Writing is an encounter between, or a union of, a masculine ascendency of will and shaping intelligence, and a native feminine topography of emotion and image. Heaney, for whom words are music before they are discourse, would no doubt characterize himself as working primarily in this "feminine" mode, where

> the language functions more as evocation than as address, and the poetic effort is not so much a labour of design as it is an act of divination and revelation; words in the feminine mode behave with the lover's come-hither instead of the athlete's display, they constitute a poetry that is delicious as texture before it is recognized as architectonic.

We may be uncomfortable with Heaney's old-fashioned terms, but they do remind us that he has continually tried to adjust our view of his work away from its pretexts and argument and towards its texture, that soft way in which experience is lined with language. And if by "feminine" we understand a Wordsworthian "wise passivity," a nurturing of "the buried life of feelings," then we are closer to Heaney's reasons for abjuring any hard political line. He has been less a poet of ideas than of place, less a poet of the heights than of the hearth. Or perhaps it would be more accurate still to say that he is a poet of the *body*, fascinated by physicality, the world's body of remembered places, the feel and scent and sound of the beloved. If Yeats found a style to resist his surroundings, Heaney has found one to savor and celebrate his.

Poetry is not printout, never merely a fading duplicate of experience. Instead, as he says in a later collection of essays, *The Redress of Poetry* (1995), a poem is the imagined alternative: "if our given experience is a labyrinth, its impassability can still be countered by the poet's imagining some equivalent of the labyrinth and situating himself and us at a point where it can be contemplated." Reading, then, is a fable about crossing from one dimension of reality to another. Poetry's counter-reality, furthermore, is meant to complicate experience rather than simplify it, to distort in order to reveal. Grotesque or ecstatic, its excess is meant to balance "life's inadequacies, desolations and atrocities," without being expected to declare ethical obligations or political motives.

His first principle is pleasure. After all, "no honest reader of poems . . . would see moral improvement or, for that matter, political education, as the end and purpose of his or her absorption in a poetic text." The pleasure we take in poems—even our guilty pleasure in poems written by a talented "oppressor" (the rhetoric, say, of colonialist England)—comes from their sensuous bravura, from their ability to include what Rilke once called "the side of life that is turned away from us," and, finally, from their instinct to transform the circumstances and conditions of life.

His second principle is nostalgia. When that note thrums beneath his poems, it serves to remind those who hear it of how often he writes—still, always—as the outsider, the "inner émigré." Like Sweeney, the poet's rhymesake and mythological king-turned-bird keening in the treetops, and also like his master James Joyce, Heaney is an exile. In his case, it is an exile from the country to the city, from the community into the writer's solitude, from the solipsism of childhood into the mortal distractions of adulthood. At his best, Heaney is the plaintive rhapsodist of that exile. He is primarily an elegiac miniaturist, a lyric poet with an impeccable ear and astonishing gifts for the surprising word, the heartstopping phrase. At the start his lyre was strung very tautly, and a little primly. In *Field Work* (1979), he relaxed his line, and also broadened the appeal of his work. He had learned, as he later said of his book, "to trust melody, to trust art as reality, to trust artfulness as an affirmation." The political poems at the front of the book, among his very best, yield to domestic and pastoral subjects that affirm the restorative power of the quotidian and of the natural world.

What he did next, in *Station Island* (1985), was pitch these same themes higher, and reverse his emphasis. The title poem sets out to be the long poem about the matter of Ireland that many of Heaney's readers—especially Americans, with their appetite for ambition and risk—must have longed for. It is a stunning piece of work, richly and dramatically imagined, if not altogether the large-scale triumph some wanted or claimed. Perhaps even more to be pondered and praised is the book's concluding sequence, "Sweeney Redivivus," a series of sometimes hermetic but always exquisite lyrics that eerily blend moments of Heaney's own past—early joys and sorrows, his loss of faith, his acquired art— with the voice of the legendary bird-king hero. This group parallels the "Bog sequence" in *North* that first brought Heaney fame but is composed with much more originality, discernment, and tender authority. It declares that here is a poet who, having mastered the traditions, might now set out to change them over in his own image. In this book of changes, he proved that a new "spirit broke cover / to raise a dust / in the front of exhaustion."

Those whose expectations for Heaney's subsequent books have thereby been raised are likely to find them something of a disappointment. Take the first of them, *The Haw Lantern*, published in 1987. I would say it had been written with damp powder, except for my lingering suspicion that the poet himself may deliberately have wanted at that point in his career, by means of this rather slight book of mostly occasional poems, to defuse again the megaton reputation many had made for him. The presiding figure in the book, the haw lantern itself, is described as a "small light," a humble red hip on its twig, glad of "not having to blind them with illumination."

On the other hand, I do not want to underrate Heaney's remarkable gifts, or the many fine poems here. The book has a heady variety: ballad and translation, riddle and dramatic monologue, complaint, blessing, eulogy, dream vision, love poem. Everywhere he writes with a cadenced ease. Consider this last part of "Hailstones," the memory of a sudden storm of childhood:

Nipple and hive, bite-lumps,
small acorns of the almost pleasurable
intimated and disallowed

when the shower ended
and everything said *wait*.
For what? For forty years

to say there, there you had
the truest foretaste of your aftermath—
in that dilation

when the light opened in silence
and a car with wipers going still
laid perfect tracks in the slush.

The sensations are tangibly described, yet still shot through with symbolic lights. The flintlike Anglo-Saxon words give way to softer Latinate terms, just as the experiment itself sinks into thought, and as the child's primary world gives way to the old heart's persuasions. Then, at the end, its epiphany earned, how convincingly he turns the poem back in on itself—the memory of tire tracks having become the very poem we're reading.

The Haw Lantern opens with other poems about childhood, not so much evocations as little preludes about the growth of the poet's mind. He is concerned with how the child he was came to words and stories, and so to a magical view of the world, subject to spells and transformation—to poetry itself. The poet John Montague once said that the whole Irish landscape is a manuscript its people have lost the skill to read. Whenever Heaney writes about the countryside, he treats it as a text. It comes as no surprise that here he maps his language as well.

This concern with language is continued in the book's half-dozen allegorical poems. These were a new route for Heaney. With titles like "From the Republic of Conscience" and "From the Canton of Expectation," they are not specific historical accounts, but meditations on spiritual conditions in a menacing political climate. They have fictive energy, but can seem vague in effect. The purpose of allegory, wrote Coleridge, is to convey in disguise "either moral qualities or conceptions of the mind that are not in themselves objects of the senses," so that their difference is everywhere present to the eye, and their likeness suggested to the imagination. The most vivid of Heaney's parables returns to the subject of a poem in an earlier collection—getting stopped in his car by a border patrol. Now it's become a version of the writer's—any writer's—imperilled conscience:

> So you drive on to the frontier of writing
> where it happens again. The guns on tripods;
> the sergeant with his on-off mike repeating
>
> data about you, waiting for the squawk
> of the clearance; the marksman training down
> out of the sun upon you like a hawk.
>
> And suddenly you're through, arraigned yet freed,
> as if you'd passed from behind a waterfall
> on the back current of a tarmac road

past armour-plated vehicles, out between
the posted soldiers flowing and receding
like tree shadows into the polished windscreen.

The heart of the book is, as before, elegiac. One of the most affecting poems is his tribute to Robert Fitzgerald, on whose death in 1984 Heaney succeeded to the Boylston professorship at Harvard. "In Memoriam: Robert Fitzgerald" uses that great translator's own Homeric figures to render a homage passionate in its restraint. Here is the conclusion, Fitzgerald's death portrayed as his hero's moment of victory:

After the bowstring sang a swallow's note,
The arrow whose migration is its mark
Leaves a whispered breath in every socket.
The great test over, while the gut's still humming,
This time it travels out of all knowing
Perfectly aimed towards the vacant centre.

The book's centerpiece is "Clearances," a sequence of eight sonnets, plus a prayer written in memory of Heaney's mother. They will recall the ten brimming "Glanmore Sonnets" in *Field Work*, which taught the hedge-school lessons of an idealized farm life. Because of its subject, "Clearances" is more austere. Anecdotal memories of his mother have the stillness of genre scenes:

When all the others were away at Mass
I was all hers as we peeled potatoes.
They broke the silence, let fall one by one
Like solder weeping off the soldering iron:
Cold comforts set between us, things to share
Gleaming in a bucket of clean water.
And again let fall. Little pleasant splashes
From each other's work would bring us to our senses.

His mother is portrayed as a rather stern and simple woman. Neither mother nor son much understand "each other's work." At home he would "decently relapse into the wrong / Grammar which kept us allied at bay," while she seems to have had a secret respect for words and his way with them. At her deathbed:

The space we stood around had been emptied
Into us to keep, it penetrated
Clearances that suddenly stood open.

These are difficult scenes and feelings to write about, much harder certainly than any political issue. Heaney's reined-in emotion is all the more wrenching. When, in the final sonnet, the heft and hush of a felled tree have become "a bright nowhere, / A soul ramifying and forever / Silent, beyond silence listened for," we are in the presence of a poet with his ear to the heart of things.

14 . C H I S E L L E D B R E A T H

?

?

?

?

?

?

?

?

?

?

When Richard Wilbur's *New and Collected Poems* appeared in 1988—and was ?
awarded the Pulitzer Prize (his second) the following year—it was the occasion
for a backward glance over an exceptional career. Because a dozen years had ?
passed since Wilbur's last book of poems, a reader's attention was naturally
drawn first to the new work added to the collected earlier. Given pride of place ?
in the book, it is a now familiar blend of his gifts for elegant lyricism, intellectual
poise, and moral sympathy. What other poet since Frost or MacLeish could
bring off such a convincing public poem—full-throated and vividly detailed ora-
tory sustained by a trenchant historical imagination—as his "On Freedom's
Ground," the text for William Schuman's cantata to honor the Statue of Liberty?
And no poet since J. V. Cunningham could have contrived so gracefully devas-
tating an epigram as Wilbur's "On Having Mis-Identified a Wild Flower:"

A thrush, because I'd been wrong,
Burst rightly into song
In a world not vague, not lonely,
Not governed by me only.

There are dreams and riddles here, satires and nature studies, a few expert translations, a poignant elegy for Auden, even a grandly clever poem about those words (*edile, esker, Elia,* and their ilk) that appear only in crossword puzzles. But best of all is "Lying," an eighty-five-line meditation that opens with the same deceptive casualness it describes: "To claim, at a dead party, to have spotted a grackle, / When in fact you haven't of late, can do no harm." From there the poet goes on, through anecdote and allusion, through all manner of lies, on to "the great lies with the eyes half-shut / That have the truth in view." Since all things are somewhere, somehow true, there are, strictly speaking, no lies. "And so with that most rare conception, nothing. / What is it, after all, but something missed?" Yet Wilbur's theme is precisely this Stevensian "nothing that is," insinuating itself into our thoughts, our souls, ever since "the garden where we first mislaid / Simplicity of wish and will." "Lying" joins a trio of other poems from earlier collections—"In Limbo," "The Mind-Reader," and "Walking to Sleep"—that brood on in-between states, the borders of consciousness. They are looser, longer than Wilbur's other poems, tentative explorations rather than cogent summaries, and they show to best advantage his dramatic abilities and mastery of psychological nuance that in other, more formally rigorous poems are concentrated in a single image. Given the eerie power of their effect, I wish there had been more such poems during his career. But, however well he works on the edge, he has been more comfortable at the balanced center of things. On the other hand, he has deliberately ruled out so much—free verse, the long poem, obscurity and slovenly autobiography, extremes of subject or emotion—that his is actually one of the most difficult sorts of poetry to write these days. If he is a poet of the middle state, such self-imposed restraints (preferences or instincts, he would call them) are no less challenging to the writer. Having been found in a grain of sand, eternity may be the more mysterious. The final lines of another of the new poems in this book, "Icarium Mare," describe his ambition succinctly:

This is no outer dark
But a small province haunted by the good,
    Where something may be understood
And where, within the sun's coronal arc,

We keep our proper range,
Aspiring, with this lesser globe of sight,
    To gather tokens of the light
Not in the bullion, but in the loose change.

That last phrase recalls the title of Wilbur's first collection, *The Beautiful Changes*. In 1947, where other poets sounded merely drab or portentous, his work stood out as brightly intellectual and brilliantly turned. He delighted in a "maculate, cracked, askew, / Gay-pocked and potsherd world" of objects and ideas—the *fallen* world, in short, of the religious imagination that yearns for transcendence but works out its salvation among the jagged edges of scattered, flashing bits of a mirrored life. As his subsequent books appeared, it became clear that his abiding subject is desire, "the dreamt land / Toward which all hungers leap, all pleasures pass." The object of that desire is often a white goddess. As lover, mate, muse, or stranger, the beloved female figure haunts many of his poems. I am thinking of such poems as "Complaint," "A Late Aubade," "She," "To Ishtar," "Piazza di Spagna, Early Morning," "Apology," and half a dozen more. Wonder more than passion is the note these poems sound. The woman in them is a luminous presence against which so much masculine darkness or confusion stands out. The textures of Wilbur's celebrations are everywhere luxuriant, and such sensuality is missing from most modern poetry.

But his desire is also embodied in the landscape and in weather. Rural epiphanies abound, and they serve the purposes both of observation and private revelation. "The heart's wish for life" is over and over again projected onto New England scenes of volatile seasonal changes or surprising urges from underground or overhead. A loneliness haunts these poems too. Like Adam east of Eden, this poet is only "hopelessly at home." He writes with the understanding that love and beauty imply a separation. The detached observer in a forest clearing, or the lover awakened by dawn—both share the same ache:

And call that sorrow sweet
That teaches us to see
The final face of love
In what we cannot be.

Certain poems from Wilbur's early books were quickly anthologized and became standards, as firmly implanted as some of Donne or Shelley. Readers and writers of my generation cut their teeth on them, but later those same models seemed to be a despised rallying point for opponents from every new fashion to campaign against. Wilbur himself, above the fray and perhaps fading from critical attention, seemed impervious to fashions, whether Beat or confessional, expressionist or minimalist or demotic. But, of course, his work did change and grow in authority, as is clear from reading this big book. Through the years he consistently wrote in a style that flattered the mind his poems celebrated—its powers and limits. But read today, his early poems often strike the ear as quaint. They are written in a rather stagey dialect of their own, one that prefers "fane" to "grove," or "espial" to "sight." He clearly wanted a sort of "poetic diction" that would resist the ordinary and sacrifice neither clarity nor nuance. Yeats and Auden prompted him, to be sure, but the example of two poets has been crucial to his work from the start: Milton and Frost. He may not be a temperamentally suitable model, but the sinuosity, the Latinate cast and lexical complexities of Wilbur's poems owe much to Milton. Frost is the more obvious tutor. The newest poems in this collection still try, as the early ones did, for Frost's buoyant speechliness. "Orchard Trees, January," for instance, opens this way: "It's not the case, though some might wish it so / Who from a window watch the blizzard blow."

Verse and speech, then, compete within the metrical bounds of his poems. So do two other impulses. One is a strongly moralizing tone that pulls his poems inward toward a clinching abstraction. The other is a dramatic flair that varies and extends his ideas outward into narrative and images. In his very best poems, these are complementary impulses. But over the years, he has come to favor the dramatic. It is not that he shies from rational argument, but he weaves now with a thicker, more homespun wool, and in rather less intricate patterns. The poems that result are even more appealing. And I don't think critics have sufficiently noted Wilbur's extraordinary command of small details, which have a prominent place in his later poems. In a brook, he watches "A startled inchling trout / Of spotted near-transparency, / Trawling a shadow solider than he." The fall twilight "darkens like a fast-reducing broth, / Simmering the shape of things." At a party, "the beaked ladle plies the chuckling ice." Everything has been minutely scrutinized and described with a precision that can startle. And he makes of these details, in gestures stately or homely, many memorable images. Sea waves suddenly become horses that have slipped their lunar reins. Or, at an exotic bird market, the cages come to stand for love, the "one outrageous need":

> We love the small, said Burke. And if the small
> Be not yet small enough, why then by Hell
> We'll cramp it till it knows but how to feed,
> And we'll provide the water and the seed.

Whole poems can be organized by such details. Let me quote a brief one. "For W. H. Auden," in a single long sentence, unfolds its understanding by a series of vignettes that invoke Auden's own concerns—not as ideas but as characters, a catalogue with the specific gravity of any lines of Whitman. The innocence of each becomes a touching figure for the vulnerability of human life. And because, by the end, Auden himself has turned into the very poems he'd made, Wilbur is discretely extending an elegiac tradition Auden had honored with *his* poem on Yeats's death:

> Now I am surer where they were going,
> The brakie loping the tops of the moving freight,
> The beautiful girls in their outboard, waving to someone
> As the stern dug in and the wake pleated the water,
>
> The uniformed children led by a nun
> Through the terminal's uproar, the dew-drawn scholar descending
> The cast-iron stair of the stacks, shuffling his papers,
> The Indians, two to a blanket, passing in darkness,
>
> Also the German prisoner switching
> His dusty neck as the truck backfired and started—
> Of all these noted in stride and detained in memory
> I now know better that they were going to die,
>
> Since you, who sustained the civil tongue
> In a scattering time, and were poet of all our cities,
> Have for all your clever difference quietly left us,
> As we might have known you would, by that common door.

This *New and Collected Poems* also provided us with the chance to test our old reactions to Wilbur's work. Though there are many other poems here that will delight readers and instruct new writers, I want to offer my own short list of those poems central to our understanding and appreciation of Wilbur's career: "Praise in Summer," "Water Walker," "Cicadas" (formerly "Cigales"), "Giacometti," "Clearness," "Grasse: The Olive Trees," " 'A World Without Objects Is a Sensible Emptiness,' " "A Baroque Wall-Fountain in the Villa Sciarra," "Looking Into History," "After the Last Bulletins," "Love Calls Us to the Things of This World," "Fall in Corrales," "The Undead," "Advice to a Prophet," "Walking to Sleep," "The Agent," "On the Marginal Way," "The Mind-Reader," "The Fourth of July," "In Limbo," "A Storm in April," "Shad-Time," "For W. H. Auden," and "Lying."

An enviable list. If there is sometimes too much varnish, the draftsmanship is always impeccable, the composition noble, the coloring warm and affecting. "What is written without effort is in general read without pleasure," said Dr. Johnson. The complex disciplines of verse have always intrigued Wilbur. "A lot of my poems are arguments against a thingless, an earthless kind of imagination, or spirituality," he once told an interviewer. "I like resistance. I like it in art, as Gautier did: 'vers, marbre, onyx, émail.' And I like the world to resist my ordering of it, so that I can feel it is real and that I'm honoring its reality." To equate verse with marble or enamel says something about the polished finish of a Wilbur poem, but underestimates the pulsing, vivid movement of thought and feeling that goes on inside the poem. Wilbur's poems do not especially gain by being read in bulk—as, say, Lowell's do. Each of his best poems is a richness to be savored, not gobbled with the rest. But this collection is a welcome convenience, and I hope it helps discourage those readers who with faint praise classify Wilbur as merely a representative poet, the spokesman for a period or an aesthetic. There are poems throughout the book that will take any preconception by surprise, poems—we realize with sudden joy—that we've had in mind and by heart for years, the first sign that a book is likely to remain a classic. Or, as the poet himself once put it, with characteristic understatement, "I should like to be thought of as someone who wrote two or three poems which, as Robert Frost said, have been 'hard to get rid of.' "

15. Sitting Here Strangely On Top of the Sunlight

?

?

?

?

?

?

?

?

?

?

?

?

?

?

At the height of his fame, from the 1963 publication of his watershed collection *The Branch Will Not Break* until his death in 1980, James Wright was revered as a master for all the wrong reasons. A legion of untalented imitators needed a strong model to distort; ideologues wanted a prophetic voice in their imagined wilderness. Wright was hailed for having shed the ill-fitting singing robes, cut from heavy rhetorical brocade, that he wore in his first two books, and for next conjuring the numinous pieties of the natural world and the dark deputies of unreason into poems with a sudden spiritual depth and stark originality.

This account of his career used to get on Wright's nerves. He would repeat to interviewers that he considered himself a traditionalist, a Horatian, that he had always clung to a fastidious neo-classical ideal. Poems of his that sound surrealist, he insisted, were simply evidence "that my attempt to be clear has failed." Critics who praised him as a political poet mistook his decorous privacy of vision. To those who acclaimed him an innovator, he replied that he was a conservative. He regarded iambic verse and free verse not as opposed but as complementary formal schemes; what others thought of as his radical rejection of an early allegiance to formal verse, he maintained was the effort to extend the formal possibilities of the American language. Lucidity, precision, rhythmical poise, sentiment, intelligence, and the rigors of a conscious craft that liberated the imagination—these were the poetic values he cherished, and they remain the keynotes of his collected poems, *Above the River*, published in 1992.

Curiously, these qualities are harder to see now in his early poems, written in imitation of the strict meters and tragic ironies of Edwin Arlington Robinson and Robert Frost. Wright wanted, he wrote about these poems, to "say something humanly important instead of just showing off with language." But there is a good deal of showing off, and Wright's language now sounds dated. A period quality—the period of the late fifties—suffuses its elevated tone and cautious rhymes.

On the other hand, Wright tried for something few of his peers attempted. He used the strategies of his formal verse to help each poem enact a moral choice, and he brought that moral attention to bear on a subject familiar from the Romantic poets—the social outcast. In *The Green Wall* (1957) and especially in *Saint Judas* (1959), his poems address their sympathies to murderer, prostitute, lesbian, lunatic, a deaf child—the whole underclass of fifties exclusion. In the title poem of *Saint Judas*, for instance, Wright wants to rescue even the most notorious traitor. His Judas, despairing and in flight from his own treachery, comes upon a man attacked by hoodlums:

> Banished from heaven, I found this victim beaten,
> Stripped, kneed, and left to cry. Dropping my rope
> Aside, I ran, ignored the uniforms:
> Then I remembered bread my flesh had eaten,
> The kiss that ate my flesh. Flayed without hope,
> I held the man for nothing in my arms.

The best of his early poems hover over such scenes—victims in the arms of other victims, with their broken lives, baffled love, wasted chances. In the hindsight this collected edition allows, though, the true focus of Wright's sympathies is clearer. There are moments when his pity is unsparing: "I would not raise you smooth and pure: / I would bare to heaven your uncommon pain." And to an interviewer Wright once confessed that his famed compassion was more often just fear. What he identifies himself with is not so much the suffering of these victims as their isolation. Their lives are the "dirt of my flesh, defeated, underground." *Loneliness* recurs more often than any other word in Wright's work, but the better term is *aloneness*, the harrowing sense of being forever a man apart.

Two traditional consolations for this felt sense of spiritual desolation are the natural world and love. It was to the former that Wright turned in his next book, *The Branch Will Not Break* (1963), the single best book of his career and an example crucial to the experimental mood of the sixties. At the time, the book seemed an abrupt reversal of his early intentions and style. Possibilities had replaced prescriptions. Instead of an elaborate verse, he relied on open forms and speech rhythms, on dreamily disjunctive "deep images" meant to release buried energies. I prefer these poems to Wright's earlier, more formal work, but I do not pretend they are any less literary. Perhaps his best-known poem from this period, "Lying in a Hammock," contemplates an afternoon with a detached intensity that is almost Chinese. Cowbells, pines, a circling hawk—and then a sudden, piercing realization: "I have wasted my life." That epiphany's random shock effect may distract readers both from its echo of Rilke and from other, very traditional details. The poem opens casually: "Over my head, I see the bronze butterfly." But as an emblem of the poet's desires, Wright's bronze butterfly is no different than Yeats's golden nightingale.

Half a dozen poems in *The Branch Will Not Break* will remain classics. Less discursive but more intellectually challenging than his early work, these pastoral poems of his middle period reveal Wright's essentially lyric imagination. Though he begins in this book to address historical issues, he clearly moves from moral to aesthetic preoccupations. Even the abandoned mills and tenement whorehouses, the suckholes and freight cars of his native Ohio—images our great photographers have already made familiar to us—have in Wright's spare poems the beauty of old engravings of classical ruins. And I wonder now if his abiding fascination with the powers of transformation, beginning with his own command of metaphor, doesn't again have to do with the struggle to escape his aloneness. In "The Jewel," for instance, the Keatsian luxuriance of the poem's imagery is drawn over an emptiness, over a sense of mortality the poet longs to transcend:

There is a cave
In the air behind my body
That nobody is going to touch:
A cloister, a silence

Closing around a blossom of fire.
When I stand upright in the wind,
My bones turn to dark emeralds.

The second half of Wright's career witnessed a grievous slump in his powers. The new work in his earlier *Collected Poems* (1971), all of *Two Citizens*
(1973), and most of *To a Blossoming Pear Tree* (1977) are ramshackle and self-
pitying. Mooning over "my rotted Ohio" or the brutalities of American policy,
Wright yields to an unaccustomed bluster. All along, it had been his poetic
task to explore his own—and, hence, our—capacity to *feel*. His tender images
were meant to evoke, restore, even redeem our emotional lives, however those
lives may have been gutted by failure. The risk Wright always ran was senti-
mentality, and too much of his later work is merely cloying.

A poignant recovery, though, occurred at the end. Wright's last collection,
This Journey, virtually assembled on his deathbed and published posthumously in 1982, dwells on small things (a field mouse, a lizard, a shell) and is
the most Horatian of his books—if by that term we mean what Auden meant:
to look on the world with a happy eye, but from a sober perspective. At the
heart of this late romance are love and the green world. His early books are
haunted by Jenny, a drowned prostitute he loved and could not save. Now, his
beloved second wife, Annie, who saved him, figures as his muse. "The friendship of daylight / And a little peace" that Wright had sought in Italy and southern France, where many of these last poems are set, recapture the imaginary
edenic world of his first vision.

Look, the sea has not fallen and broken
Our heads. How can I feel so warm
Here in the dead center of January? I can
Scarcely believe it, and yet I have to, this is
The only life I have. I get up from the stone.
My body mumbles something unseemly
And follows me. Now we are all sitting here strangely
On top of the sunlight.

In an essay about Whitman written nearly forty years ago, Wright tried to
counter the then prevailing notion of Whitman as one of the poetic roughs.
Instead, he insisted on Whitman's *delicacy*, on his sensitivity to a rare music

beyond the ordinary, on a restraint, clarity, and wholeness that together embody a spiritual inwardness. This more accurately serves as a description of Wright himself. Of course he lacked Whitman's magnitude. The narrowed range of Wright's characteristic subjects and format, the very delicacy of his instincts, confine him. But his best poems, with their grace and intelligence, not only stood as a rebuke to most of the glib work of his time, but remain among the finest examples of the mid-century American lyric. His poems continue, as a phrase from one of them puts it, to break into blossom.

16 . THE LOST UPLAND

The Languedoc region of southwest France has a worn-down ruggedness to it.
In the squares of its small towns, the old men play boules and sip pastis. The
countryside is fissured limestone and rusted signposts, groves of gnarled plum
and walnut trees, pigeon towers, raindrops plumped with green light, the ton-
kle of sheep bells, hay wagons, slate roofs, boar and wren and eglantine. In
1954, with the help of an eight-hundred-dollar legacy from an old school-
teacher aunt, W. S. Merwin bought a stone farmhouse in the Quercy. It turned
out to be the best investment of his life. His imagination has lived off the interest ever since, in poems and memoirs. A collection of his stories based on the
region, *The Lost Upland*, was published in 1992 to rapturous praise. *The
Vixen*—published in 1996, the fifteenth collection of his career—returns to
both this landscape and his memories of it. The book is not just a gathering of
miscellaneous poems, but a single tapestry of images woven into an allegory of
Loss. To the extent that it evokes a place, a period in his life, the book is suffused with details of country life—solitary walks and garden work,

woodsmoke, birdsong, lightfall. To the extent that is about memory itself, the book turns that place into a myth, a lost paradise.

This is not another of those now popular books about a bemused outsider's sojourn in rural France, brimming with colorful locals and heartwarming anecdotes. There are a few people in *The Vixen*—historical characters of the region, a couple of aged neighbors named Esther and Edouard, Richard the mason, a "you," an "us." But there are more ghosts than people. The book begins with the figure of a ghost—a fox in the shape of an old man—and ghosts abound throughout. Merwin himself is a spectral presence here, walking back through the vanished landscape of his own past. The popular books trade in nostalgia. Merwin's poems are elegies. And melancholy's sweet-and-sour tributes to a place, in the end, have everything to do with the self. The way we remember is, of course, the way we also forget. This poet is keenly aware of how the past eludes us, of how much we discard, the better to cherish whatever we sense may still feed our desires. His evocations are at once a homage to the past and a defense against both the chaos of the passing moment and the blankness of the future. And at the heart of Merwin's book is a persistent ache. "Did I think it would abide as it was forever / all that time ago the turned earth in the old garden / where I stood in spring remembering spring in another place / that had ceased to exist."

One has to lean forward to hear these quiet poems. They sound much the same way Stravinsky described the sound of a guitar: not small, but as if from far away. And because Merwin eschews standard punctuation, one sometimes strains to follow him, reading a phrase both forward and backward to track its fluctuating syntactical status. His lines can seem like silk panels moved by invisible hands—crossing, overlapping, changing suddenly but imperceptibly a color or a mood. Merwin's poems are not vessels to contain meaning, but nets to catch new meanings as they drift through the lines on successive readings. Settled loosely on the page as on a slide, each poem is a sort of solution in which ideas float, detach, combine.

In his introduction to Merwin's first book, *A Mask for Janus*, published in 1952 as part of the Yale Younger Poets series, W. H. Auden singled out the poet's "admirable respect for the traditions of poetic craftsmanship." But Auden knew as well that skill is a prerequisite, not a goal, and he sensed something more ambitious stirring in Merwin's early work. Further along in his introduction,

Auden makes a distinction between two kinds of poem: the occasional (where a specific experience is prominent and its universal significance implied) and the mythological (whose overt subject is impersonal and universal, and the personal experience of the poet that gave rise to it is implied). Merwin he found to be a grand example of the mythological poet. And though the young poet's very next book was almost defiantly autobiographical, the truth of Auden's remark has been borne out, if by "myth" we mean not just stories of gods and beasts but gods and beasts as metaphors of the inner life, powers that control or liberate us, that help us make sense of the world—or, in Merwin's own formulation, "intuitions of a kind of coherent sense of experience, which we can't live without."

Merwin's myths themselves, over the years, have been transformed into all sorts of parables—of emptiness and exploitation, of awe and ardor. And they have helped define two stages in his career, years of the vision and years of the dream. The poems of his middle years—the poems in *The Lice* (1967) and *The Carrier of Ladders* (1970), the poems that brought him fame, and remain among the most extraordinary poems of the age—are uncanny and disquieting. Haunted by the war in Vietnam, and by capitalism's greedy assault on the environment, these books have a postapocalyptic tone. Their first readers were taken out of themselves and forced to look back on what their kind had done and had not done. There are some poets—Shakespeare, Keats, Browning, Stevens—whom we admire for their transcendent art as it plays over all the embossed surfaces of human life. But there are others—Blake, Wordsworth, Whitman, Dickinson—who we feel were granted a vision, access to the other side of experience. It is impossible to read *The Lice* and not feel that Merwin is one of this visionary company.

His most recent books, no less powerfully, pursue a dream rather than a vision, and thereby seem more richly plangent. They are as concerned with ancestors and animals, trees and tribes as his earlier books, but in a different register. A poem in *The Vixen* called "White Morning" epitomizes this tone. It is a misty morning; the poet is on a walk, and picks up a fallen bough, as any hiker might, or as someone in an old myth might . . .

> and I was holding a thin
> wet branch wrapped in lichens because all I had thought
> I knew had to be passed from branch to branch through the empty

sky and whatever I reached then and could recognize
  moved toward me out of the cloud and was still the sky
where I went on looking until I was standing on
  the wide wall along the lane to the hazel grove
where we went one day to cut handles that would last
  the crows were calling around me to white air
I could hear their wings dripping and hear small birds with lights
  breaking in their tongues the cold soaked through me I was able
after that morning to believe stories that once
  would have been closed to me I saw a carriage go under
the oaks there in full day and vanish I watched animals there
  I sat with friends in the shade they have all disappeared
most of the stories have to do with vanishing

How easily the poet maneuvers here between the present and the past, each a passage into the other. His incantatory voice enlarges the incident, and his placement of details, crow or carriage, edges them toward a mysterious symbolism. Memory itself becomes a familiar but evanescent story.

So many of his poems now dream of some lost upland, long for what has vanished, try to complete something that is felt to be incomplete. He has always been a contemplative poet, drawn to the lessons of the natural world and the rigors of the unmediated vision. He has also been—and this is uncommon in our raw, ironic century—a romantic poet, heroic in his quest for the depths and intensities, the powers and possibilities of consciousness. Best of all, he has been a surprising poet, continually finding the loophole in anyone's easy admiration. His imitators, for whom Merwin is an icon of instinct and experimentation, are deaf to the bracing intelligence and deep love of tradition that guide his imagination. Readers who want to claim him for the surrealist camp seem blind to the fact that he doesn't just string things along, has no interest in the banal or outré, and has always cared about the *shape* of a poem—which is to say that his poems have a moral purpose at their heart. All along, his originality—and he writes with one of the most distinctive and original voices in American poetry—has had to do with origins, "the place," he has said, "where something comes from, not the fact that it is different from everything else. True originality has to do not with trying to be new but trying to come from the place from which all renewal comes." In his case, that has been his vision of horrors and blessings, his dream of a lost upland. Thoreau once said of a writer, "if you can speak what you will never hear, if you can write what you will never read, you have done rare things." As *The Vixen* again shows, W. S. Merwin has done rare things indeed.

1 7 . ENCOUNTERING THE SUBLIME

?

?

?

?

?

?

?

?

?

?

I remember a time in the mid-seventies when I felt as if I were part of a last- ?
century crowd at the docks in, say, Philadelphia, waiting for the ship to land
with the next installment of the latest Dickens novel. While I passed the sum- ?
mer in Connecticut and James Merrill was in Athens, he would send me—
twenty or thirty pages every couple of weeks, hot off the Selectric but already ?
emended in ballpoint—swatches of the long poem that eventually became ?
Mirabell: Books of Number, published finally in 1978, a successor to "The
Book of Ephraim" that appeared in his 1976 volume Divine Comedies. He ?
didn't know then that Mirabell was to be only the second part of a still longer
poem, and a couple of years after I recall getting in the mail thick manila ?
envelopes with pages from what was then turning into Scripts for the Pageant,
published in 1980. Two years later, he gathered all three poems, added a
coda, and assembled his trilogy into a single volume, The Changing Light at
Sandover, a poem at once private and epic, occult and humane. For me, getting the poem in bits, kept in suspense, editing and arguing with the text, was
the ideal way to read such a sprawling, ambitious work. It allowed me time

to absorb its givens—the Ouija board paraphernalia, the huge cast of characters, the shifting perspectives and tones. While he was writing *Scripts*, he had isolated himself in his apartment, high over the harbor in Stonington, Connecticut; he didn't go out or have people in, made few phone calls, rose at dawn and worked at his desk all day and into the night—all of it uncharacteristic behavior. His close friends realized that he was in the grip of something, and that "something" was, yes, a poem, but more than a poem: a task, a vision.

No more than his readers could the poet himself see exactly where he was going as he was prompted by revelations and injunctions from Beyond and by the shape-shifting nature of the text he was fashioning from the raw transcripts of his sessions at the Ouija board with his companion, David Jackson. And in a similar manner, it is hard to say now whether history will consider *The Changing Light* to have been the masterwork of his career or a glorious curiosity. It will not, however, be ignored, for it contains every impulse of his imagination, every gesture and theme found elsewhere in his books. But here they are skewed, disguised, enlarged, drawn out and up into a panoply of enormous proportions and consequence. It is as if his poetic career had enacted the classical progression, and moved from the lyric to the epic, from the pastorals of lost love and foreign landscapes to the more austere grandeurs of the long poem, the mighty line. With a self-deprecating crack, Merrill himself once referred to it as a case of "middle-age spread," but that was meant wittily to shrug off a heavy burden. Like Virgil or Milton, Pope or Tennyson before him, Merrill had assumed the epic mantle. And his seeming reluctance to do so is what gives his poem its distinctive edge. I want to take a closer look now at both that burden and that reluctance.

Just as what Merrill calls the "vital" settings of *The Changing Light at Sandover* shift—from Stonington to Athens to Venice; from salon to seminar, tribunal to parade—so too is the lifeblood of his poem its mingling of genres. The structural designs, the tonal registers, and the leading motifs of half a dozen traditional genres are subsumed by this prodigious trilogy. In fact, Merrill's poem is precisely that hybrid form—that *ensemble*—Whitman predicted would characterize the great long poems of America. By turns and at once, *Sandover* is epic narrative, picaresque adventure, spiritual autobiography, quest romance, cosmogonic scripture or court masque, now a dramatic play of voices in the style of Goethe's *Faust*, now an instructed pilgrimage toward vision in the line of Dante's *Commedia*.

I want to single out just one strain of its burden: the sublime. One critic's persuasive first review of *Scripts for the Pageant* claimed the poem "defines the sublime for our age." I should like to agree except for my sense that, like poetry itself, the sublime is easier to recognize than to define. It is not, like epic or romance, a genre. It is a tone, but a tone raised to such a pitch that it becomes subject matter, and a subject at the height of poetic ambition. Longinus recognized it in Genesis; later readers have recognized it in Dante and Hugo, Milton and Wordsworth, Whitman and Crane. In each instance, what we recognize is that poet's encounter with imaginative power at its most intense and uncanny—"the deep power," as Emerson once called it, that is the soul's enormous claim. This power can be daemonic or divine; it may sometimes be idealized and internalized, and thereby involve the self's compensatory response to loss, as it sometimes appears in Merrill's poem; or it may be visionary and ecstatic or prophetic, as it also appears. In any case, the poet's encounter, or influx of power, is with extremes of otherness, with a transcendence beyond the reach of art and the limits of self-possession, with (as Merrill puts it in *Ephraim*) "Powers of lightness, darkness, powers that be . . . Heavens above us . . . figures of authority."

There are several such moments in the trilogy, and many more of the subsidiary contexts and effects of the sublime as that mode has come to be recognized since the eighteenth century. The awful stillness of the dictées, the occult gear and sacred precincts, passages of dread, distortions of time and space, the solemnity of "GREAT ORIGINAL IDEAS" in *Scripts*, its first and last questions and apocalyptic revelations, the dealing with nonhuman forces—I shall not inventory all of these, nor even the several crucial moments when the poet is, in his own words, imbued with otherness. Instead, I want to point to one exemplary instance. At the very end of *Mirabell*, after all the book's Gothic touches (the bats, the hurricane), after the refrains of doubts and fear, the life-and-death issues, the poem rises to a stillness that modulates from suspense to surrender. There has been a daylong vigil for the angel. In the final minutes of that "hour when Hell shall render what it owes," the sun is about to set, and an emblematic gull ascends over waters.

The message hardly needs decoding, so
Sheer the text, so innocent and fleet
These overlapping pandemonia:
Birdlife, leafplay, rockface, waterglow
Lending us their being, till the given
Moment comes to render what we owe.

The book might have ended just there. In one sense, it *should* have ended there—on the very word ("owe") that had opened the poem ("Oh, very well then"), and so completed the magician's circle the book inscribes around its revelations. But it does not end there. The shapeliness of the form is broken, and a new voice—the archangel Michael's, in long, imperious lines—commandeers the poem, replaces the voice of the poet with an "epic" voice totally other than Merrill's ("FROM THE WINEDARK SEA OF SPACE . . . "), and ends the book on an unprecedented high note of its own:

GOD IS THE ACCUMULATED INTELLIGENCE IN CELLS
    SINCE THE
DEATH OF THE FIRST DISTANT CELL
WE RESIDE IN THAT INTELLIGENCE . . .
I AM MICHAEL
I HAVE ESTABLISHED YOUR ACQUAINTANCE & ACCEPT
    YOU . . .
LOOK! LOOK INTO THE RED EYE OF YOUR GOD!

This is one of what Wordsworth names the "extraordinary calls" of the sublime—a moment such as Wordsworth himself recounts in the Mt. Snowdon passage of *The Prelude*:

There I beheld the emblem of a mind
That feeds upon infinity, that broods
Over the dark abyss, intent to hear
Its voices issuing forth to silent light
In one continuous stream; a mind sustained
By recognition of transcendent power,
In sense conducting to ideal form,
In soul of more than mortal privilege.

I might just add here that the Ouija board considered as terrain—and it is by Merrill, who even maps it—is the most compelling trope for the sublime since the rugged mountain heights of Romantic landscape, an occult sublime having replaced a "natural" sublime. This ascent to the upper case of higher meaning, this access to power comes, as in Wordsworth, at a price: the sublimation of the self. At the end of *Mirabell*, Merrill first surrenders himself to the symbolic scene's sheer text, and then surrenders his voice, or poetic control.

Such moments of obliteration and exaltation, of withdrawal and incarnation, are deeply ambivalent for this poet. They are both cultivated and resisted. It is worth stopping to recall that, in an earlier poem, "Lost in Translation," Merrill associates the word "sublime" with the word "barren." And throughout the trilogy, the *power* that JM and DJ first manifest in themselves, and then are called upon to tell of, can be a stark, even terrifying phenomenon. It is variously described as the "naked current" of the absolute, as "raw" power, a "JOY-LESS THING," as the Cosmic Mind or the Source of Light. It may be the "grand and simple" proportion of the Temple at Ephesus with its "steep and solitary path of mind," or the haunting, monochromatic tape-loop voice of God B. The daemonic muse of this sublimity is Urania, described by Michael as a "COLD & UNIVERSAL CREATURE" whose sphere is "ICY RATIONALITY." Urania, by now a familiar though elusive presence in Merrill's work, is of course the muse of Shelley, and of Milton, who invokes her in Book VII of *Paradise Lost*:

> whose voice divine
> Following, above th' Olympian hill I soar,
> Above the flight of Pegasean wing.

The lower flights of Pegasus—that peacock-and-unicorn embodiment of the imagination—is where most of this trilogy rides, below the "whirling point of Light." And the muse here is Psyche; Keats's Psyche, to be sure, and also Merrill's woman of the world, Mother Nature, who, we are told in *Scripts*, is in charge of man's "RESISTANCE, HIS 'UNGODLY' SIDE." By temperament and ambition, Merrill is not naturally a poet of the sublime—or so we might have thought before this trilogy. So *he* might have thought himself, before his emerging material impelled him to deal with a tone, a "voice

divine," that cuts through what Maria Mitsotáki in *Scripts* calls "THE IMAGE-
THWARTED PATHS BY WHICH WE THINK."

This is a topic Merrill is self-conscious about from the start. His uneasi-
ness, to a large extent, actually shapes the poem. I am thinking of the narrative concoctions of *Ephraim's* plot, or the severely repressed nonrecognition
scene with Wendell, the divine representative. How often the *telling* of the
poem, both its plot and its style, depends on just those tones that counter the
sublime, that evade or undermine it. I would mention three of them. One of
them is what used to be called the picturesque, but now ought to be called
the domestic: the distracting or enchanting details of the everyday, the trivial
necessities and accidents and collusions of a shared life—a past of their own
that JM and DJ cling to partly out of habit and partly for dear life's sake. This
is the tone that is decidedly down to earth, whether it be mundane or worldly.
When the poem's mythical undertones or divine injunctions elevate the
planchette into a holier-than-thou grail, we are quickly reminded of two
human hands on a teacup. This is the tone that quite deliberately *grounds* the
dictées in broader effects of history's lived life—sometimes that of another
homemade task, the composition (or to use the apt kitchen term, *mixing*) of
the poem itself, which continually lags behind, and so drags against, the rush
of revelation. Nor is it merely coincidental that, for the most part, the sessions
at the Ouija board occur in a dining room. This domestic tone is that of
Merrill's "CHRONICLES OF LOVE & LOSS" (and the trilogy is the grandest of these), whether of a room or a romance, an object personified or a person objectified by memory.

Second, the realistic. That is to say, a tone that accounts for boredom, separation, illness, exhaustion, anxiety, or skepticism. In section "I" of *Ephraim*,
for instance, the tone makes a scene—what we might call a countersession—
with the psychoanalyst. Or it is to be discovered in Merrill's indulgence of
what he calls Ephraim's "sense, comfort, and wit," or what in an analogous situation Wallace Stevens calls the "flippant communications" that travesty the
frigid brilliance of the great auroras. Most notably it occurs, I think, when the
poet wants, as he repeats and is enjoined, to *make sense of it*. More than common sense, to be sure. But also that. How often is the high hum of mind balanced by the poet's ear for nuance, his eye for pattern, his nose for discrepancy,
his light, sophisticated touch, and his taste for style—a *poem*—that can accommodate what it pleases and is pleased by.

And third, the sublime is countered by (so Edmund Burke told us) the beautiful. And in Merrill's case, that is synonymous with style itself, with his language's imagistic resistance to "some holy flash past words." His is a style willing to try on anything that fits—allusive, witty, ironic, tender, rhetorically complex and metrically ingenious, extremely composed and sociable—that is to say, always aware of itself addressing a subject, being attended to by an audience. The opposite, in other words, of the egotistical (or narcissistic) sublime. It is a style more comfortable with the attar of the image than with the symbol of the Rose, with sensuous detail rather than with abstract discourse or hieratic utterance. Merrill can describe his own poem (he does so late in *Ephraim*) as continually drawing him to, *and* insulating him from, the absolute, or sublime mode. What draws him toward the ineffable is language itself, its potential "depth, glimmer, and force," as he says in *Mirabell*. What insulates is the poetic diction he has fashioned from language. He is, after all—or so he's told at one point in the trilogy—part chemist and part musician.

I would like to suggest two further measures the trilogy takes against the sublime—measures no less strong for being obvious and problematic. They both have to do with the poet's role in his own poem. First, there is the fact that he has a role at all. William Blake, for instance, in a letter to Thomas Butts, said that he wrote "from immediate Dictation" by angels; that he wrote "20 or 30 lines at a time, without Premeditation and even against my Will." And in the preface to *Jerusalem*, he remarks almost casually that "when this verse was first dictated to me" his concern was what cadence to put it in, or how to make a poem from the dictation. He settled on fourteeners—but we never see him *doing* that, never see him *in* his own poem, taking the dictation or arranging it. Merrill, on the other hand, is both in character in his own poem (as JM, in the manner of Proust's Marcel), and a reader or interpreter of it, sometimes as Idiot Questioner, sometimes as structuralist critic. In *Mirabell*, he characterizes his reading self as a *doubter*, or willing unbeliever. (There is a Doubting Tom in each of the other books as well: Tom the psychoanalyst in *Ephraim*, and Tom Rakewell in *Scripts*.) This is another of the poet's strategies for anticipating his audience's hesitations, the better to disarm them, by assuming them himself, by literally incorporating them into the poem. The effect is to put a considerable distance between his subject and *its* images of the sublime. Let me put it another way. The upper-case messages, placed as they are in a larger poem that includes them in its history of the events, function as a text within the text, and have the corresponding power over JM that any text has over a reader. The sublime (like a text) demands a submission—a remission of the imagination—that Merrill (as poet) can portray without positing.

The second measure—one more fraught and therefore more exacting—is Merrill's role as *poet* within the poem. Not JM now, but James Merrill, the lower case of everything that is in this world. Let's open the case. It's a puzzling and enriching one. What we find is the primal scene of the poet in competition with his text; again, style countering the sublime. When one thinks back on the trilogy, one remembers—is meant to *remember*—the lavish set pieces: the Ode to Mercury and the terza rima Venetian interlude in *Ephraim*, the dance of the elements and the starstruck Hymn to Mother Nature in *Mirabell*, the Samos canzone, the Chant of the Square Deific, and the semidetached House in Athens, all in *Scripts*. And this is to say nothing of the dozens of ligatory sonnets and couplets, villanelles and ballads that Merrill deploys to assert his own power by insisting on its incidental triumphs, by using his transactions with the other world to frame his own mirroring genius.

To conclude, I want briefly to resume my series of contrasts in the most general way. In a sense, the trilogy is of two minds about itself—the poet's and the poem's, its struggle between shrewd crossfire upon the page and unwilled ascents, the mock-heroic interplay—or interface, if you will—of upper and lower case. When told of his affinities with the element of air in *Mirabell*, JM is further reminded that his true vocation is for "MIND & ABSTRACTION— THE REGION OF STARRY THOUGHT COOLER THAN / SWIFTER THAN / LIGHTER THAN EARTH." Yet throughout the trilogy he refuses— or wants to refuse—such a calling. His temperamental diffidence in *Ephraim* grows into a nagging reluctance in the face of the sublime task in *Mirabell*, until finally resistance itself becomes the subject of *Scripts*—indeed, its very format, YES & NO.

Merrill can be lighthearted about this, boasting in a neat pun, for instance, that one must brace the little foot against high heaven, or confessing, with almost too much stress on the word *engagingly*:

> My characters, this motley alphabet,
> Engagingly evade the cul-de-sac
> Of the Whole Point, dimensionless and black.

But Merrill knew what he was about; knew, with his guardian angel Michael, that "all forward motion knows resistance." If his long poem was not merely to be The Triumph of After-Life, then Merrill was determined from the beginning to create momentum for his story, and to sustain interest in his subject, by a middle flight between human and divine, time and eternity. He allowed equal time to Urania and Psyche. Unwilling to be just the spokesman for his visions, like Blake, Merrill built up this huge, overarching structure of delicate balances—a geodesic dome of sorts—to contain the power (the various *possessions*) the poem acquires.

In an essay, Yeats once said that the ideal poet would maintain "self-possession in self-surrender" to his material. Failing that ideal—as most do—Merrill alternated those responses, using the one to evoke the other, entrusting himself to guides who are both "protective and conductive." Such a strategy enabled him to shape and complete his poem—that is to say, draw it up, far up to a whirling point of light, and then in its Coda to ease the poem tellingly, movingly back to where it all began.

18. BRAVING THE ELEMENTS

The news that James Merrill had died (on February 6, 1995) in Arizona of a sudden heart attack at the age of sixty-eight caused a palpable shock in the literary world. Spontaneous tributes and readings sprang up at universities and gatherings around the country. Disbelieving letters and phone calls crisscrossed the circle of professional writers. Not since a grand chapter closed in the 1970s with the deaths of W. H. Auden, Robert Lowell, and Elizabeth Bishop has the loss of an American poet been as momentous, or as widely acknowledged to be so.

That is in part because, however compelling his ambitions or demanding his methods, Merrill's readers always felt a sort of intimacy. For fifty years, the poet had used the details of his own life to shape a portrait that in turn mirrored back to us the image of our world and our moment. When his sixth book of poems, *Braving the Elements*, appeared in 1972, Helen Vendler's review in the *New York Times* struck early what came to be the dominant note in appraisals of Merrill: "The time eventually comes, in a good poet's career, when readers actively long for his books: to know that someone out there is writing down your century, your generation, your life—under whatever terms of difference—makes you wish for news of yourself, for those authentic tidings of invisible things, as Wordsworth called them, that only come in the interpretation of life voiced by poetry."

For his funeral service in Stonington, on a raw February afternoon, the little village church—its whitewashed interior suddenly looking rather Greek—was filled. A piping soprano sang Bach's "Bist du bei mir" to the plaintive accompaniment of a virginal, and Merrill's good friend, the novelist Allan Gurganus, spoke a brief eulogy. "Some people contain their grace," he said. "James dispersed his. It was a molecular nimbus he lived within and he seemed, after nearly seven decades in there, largely unaware of its effervescent effect on the rest of us. How rare, when the great man is a good man." Later, at the cemetery where a mossy oblong of sod lay beside the tiny grave, a clutch of friends each sprinkled a handful of dirt over the poet's ashes. When it was his turn, one young poet also dropped into the grave a dimestore playing marble painted to resemble the globe itself.

The shock has slowly subsided for his friends into the dull realization that there will be no more of his witty company. Yes, he was a great poet and knew he was meant to end up as books on a shelf. Those twenty books have long since confirmed his mastery: he knew more about the language of poetry than anyone since Auden, and used it to make poems that will remain part of anyone's definition of the art. But so, too, his conversation. He liked, as he once said, "English in its billiard-table sense—words that have been set spinning against their own gravity." At a large dinner party or on a casual stroll, with old acquaintance or perfect stranger, he had an almost anarchic habit of turning everything upside down. By his slight adjustment of perspective, or realignment of syllable, the dire became droll. He rarely relaxed his instinctive habit of reversing a truth or upending the mawkish, and his face—with its pursed smile and arched brow—loved to anticipate the pleasure his remark was about to give.

In 1994, for instance, at a Met performance of *Otello*, the Desdemona was in trouble long before her tragic end. Carol Vaness, playing the role in her own red hair, had developed a wobble and decided to withdraw. Her cover, in a more traditional black wig, took over the last act. After the performance, making his way up the aisle, Merrill turned to a friend and shook his head with a rueful giddiness, "Poor Desdemona! She changed the color of her hair, but it didn't save her marriage."

The crack is characteristic in other ways. To begin with, he was at the opera, and nothing over the years had given him more pleasure nor at the start had taught him more. He began going to the Met when he was eleven, and one of his best-known poems, "Matinees," describes its effect: "The point thereafter was to arrange for one's / Own chills and fever, passions and betrayals, / Chiefly in order to make song of them." Opera—its ecstasies and deceptions, its transcendent fires and icy grandeurs—is above all a stylized dramatization of our inner lives, our forbidden desires and repressed fears. It may seem surprising in a poet like Merrill, whose surfaces can be so elegant and elusive, but center stage in his work is passion. However his words may work to heighten and refine it, the urgency of the heart's desires is his constant subject.

That Merrill would joke not about Desdemona's murder but about her failed marriage also points to a distant event that came to shape his imagination. At about the same time he first starting going to the opera, his parents separated. A bitter divorce trial followed, and because Merrill's father was one of the most powerful financiers in America, co-founder of the great brokerage house of Merrill Lynch, the story was front-page news. One tabloid even ran a photograph of young James with the caption "PAWN IN PARENTS' FIGHT." Again and again over the course of his career, Merrill would revisit the scene, nowhere more memorably than in his sequence of sonnets called "The Broken Home." Thirty years after the fact, the poem manages a knowing shrug: "Always that same old story— / Father Time and Mother Earth, / A marriage on the rocks." But the poem's impulse here to mythologize the trauma is part of a larger scheme. It was as if the divorce represented Merrill's own split personality. As much his father's son as his mother's boy, he had a temperament that by turns revealed what I may as well call paternal and maternal sides. He was drawn equally to the rational and the fanciful, the passionate and the ironic, idea and fact, America and Europe. And from the very beginning, his ambition as a poet had been—like the child attempting to reconcile his warring parents—to harmonize those two sides of his life. More often than not, he preferred to remain of two minds about all matters. But the energy spent exploring these divisions and doublings, all the obsessions and inventions of his work, from the delicacies of metaphor on to the creation of an entire cosmogony, fuelled a career as remarkable as any in American literary history.

As children, most of us fantasize a glamorous alternative: our parents are royal and rich, we live in a palace, we are adored and powerful. But if those happen to be the *facts* of your life instead of your fantasies? His parents had a brownstone on West 11th Street, and a stately Stanford White pile in Southampton, "The Orchard," with its dozen bedrooms, its conservatories and rose-arbors, cooks and chauffeurs. In his 1957 roman à clef, *The Seraglio*, Merrill portrays his father in his later years as a sort of pasha, surrounded by wife, ex-wives, mistresses, nurses, and flatterers, a man who loved his wives deeply but cheerlessly while counting on other women for companionship and fun. He was a man whose face "would have made the fortune of any actor. Frank, earnest, noble in repose, it was kept from plain tiresome fineness by being always on the verge of some unlikely humor, mischief or doltishness or greed." Merrill's mother, Hellen Ingram, was Charles Merrill's second wife, a Jacksonville beauty who had once been a newspaper reporter and kept close tabs on her son. It's almost natural that Merrill's childhood fantasies weren't the usual ones. If his ballad, "Days of 1935," is a fair account of them, he imagined himself kidnapped like the Lindbergh baby and carried off to some shabby hideout by a gangster and his moll with whose cheap looks—her rosebud chewing gum, his sallow, lantern-jawed menace—he falls in love and from whose violent ways he begs not to be ransomed.

"It strikes me now maybe," he told an interviewer in 1982, "that during much of my childhood I found it difficult to *believe* in the way my parents lived. They seemed so utterly taken up with engagements, obligations, ceremonies—every child must feel that, to some extent, about the grown-ups in his life." In fact, like most childhoods, his was lonely. He craved affection, and spent most of his time with an adored governess, reading up on the Norse myths or devising plots to present in his puppet theater. The loneliness—almost a necessary condition for any poet's working life—and the need to charm run right through his poems. By the time he was eight he was writing poems. By the time he was at Lawrenceville, he meant to make a career of it and told his father so. Charles Merrill, distressed by his son's determination, nonetheless took a businessman's approach. He secretly sent his son's fledgling poems and stories to three "experts," including the president of Amherst, and asked for their frank opinion of the boy's prospects. When they all agreed on a precocious talent, Merrill had a volume—called *Jim's Book*—privately printed, to the young author's immediate delight and future chagrin. The patriarch was heard to say he'd rather have a first-rate poet for a son than a third-rate stockbroker.

In his last years, Merrill had begun to notice in his shaving mirror each morning how much he had come to resemble his father. "A face no longer / sought in dreams but worn as my own" is how one poem puts it. He never thought to look for that face earlier, since the young need always to consider themselves unique. In his memoir, A *Different Person*, published in 1993, he remembers looking at himself in 1950:

> From the mirror stares inquiringly a slim person neither tall nor short, in a made-to-order suit of sandy covert cloth and a bow-tie. My bespectacled face is so young and unstretched that only by concentration do the lips close over two glinting chipmunk teeth. My hair, dark with fair highlights, is close-cropped. I have brown eyes, an unexceptionable nose, a good jaw. My brow wrinkles when I am sad or worried, as now. Not that what I see dismays me. Until recently I've been an overweight, untidy adolescent; now my image in the glass is the best I can hope for. Something, however, tells me that time will do little to improve it. The outward bloom of youth upon my features will fade long before the budlike spirit behind them opens—if ever it does. It is inside that I need to change. To this end I hope very diffidently to get away from the kind of poetry I've been writing.

The kind of poetry he was writing then—his *First Poems* appeared in 1951—was very much of its time. Merrill had been a prodigy, turning out incised, world-weary sonnets at sixteen. He began publishing his work in leading magazines at twenty. The aloof, lapidary glamour of his poems, their dissolves and emblems, were meant both to disguise feelings only dimly known and to declare his allegiance to a line of poets that could be traced from Wallace Stevens back to the Symbolistes. But before too long, he had written a novel and had a couple of plays produced off-Broadway, and from both experiences he had learned to write a more fluent and inflected line, often coaxed by narrative.

By 1954, Merrill had decided to abandon New York City. He moved with his companion David Jackson to Stonington, a small Connecticut coastal village—half fishing fleet, half Yankee clapboard—that a friend suggested might remind him of Portugal. He and Jackson bought a house; they had a brass bed, a record player, a rowboat, a table and two chairs to work on, and no telephone. He loved the light glinting on Long Island Sound, and the cozy, settled routines of village life; the town, he said, was "full of clever wrinkled semi-famous people whom by the end of our second season we couldn't live without." By 1959, he and Jackson had made another move, soon after bought another house, and for the next two decades spent half of each year in Athens.

Both moves were, in a sense, strategic withdrawals. Like his friend Elizabeth Bishop, Merrill did what he could to avoid having to lead a Literary Life. Stonington's bright calm began to give his work a more domestic focus. In the collection named for his address, *Water Street* (1962), there is a poem that speaks of his "dull need to make some kind of house / Out of the life lived, out of the love spent." Always aware that the very word *stanza* is Italian for "room," Merrill put together poems that would shelter his memories. Increasingly, his poems were autobiographical, reaching back to his childhood or puzzling over some passing event or involvement. Merrill eventually described his poems as "chronicles of love and loss," and that term aptly stresses his sense of a life lived and understood over time, and links his two recurrent themes. From his college days on, Merrill's favorite writer had been Proust, for whom the only true paradise was a lost paradise. Love, for both writers, is not fully itself until it is lost, until it becomes memory, becomes art.

If the familiarities of Stonington afforded both distance and security, Greece gave him something else. Here was a landscape of ravishing ruggedness, a culture of exotic simplicities, life on a smaller human scale. Better still, a language—he quickly mastered it—in which his accent wouldn't at once betray his class. He loved the anonymity it gave him; he loved the very sound of it: "kaló-kakó, cockatoo-raucous / Coastline of white printless coves / Already strewn with offbeat echolalia." The poems set in Greece, vivid with local color, are the highlight of his two subsequent books, *Nights and Days* (1966) and *The Fire Screen* (1969). Landscapes as different as New Mexico and Key West would later figure in his work as well. Merrill was a poet who looked out at a scene or around a room to prompt him. "I always find," he told an interviewer, "when I don't like a poem I'm writing, I don't look any more into the human components. I look more to the *setting*—a room, the objects in it." What was in front of his eyes would reveal what was in his mind. It was a quality he especially admired in the poems of Eugenio Montale, the way their ladles and love letters, their ordinary furniture and pets, led finally deep into a labyrinth of feeling.

The rooms of his Stonington house, which gave the impression of a boutique fantasque, were themselves an image of Merrill's inner life: a clutter of beloved totems. An immense Victorian mirror would reflect masterpiece and tchotchke, piles of books on the horsehair divan, a glass bowl filled with glass globes, his bat-motif wallpaper, a Maxfield Parrish, a tanagra, a snapshot of his goddaughter, a Moghul mianiature, a wooden nickel, cacti and shells, a

Meissen plate, a lacquered Japanese travelling box, a wind-up toy bird, the upheld hand of the Buddha.

A couple of years ago, Allan Gurganus wrote to Merrill, urging him to reread Tolstoy's novella, *Married Happiness*. The poet dutifully looked for it, but could only find it in French, in one of the worn Pleiade editions he kept by his bed in Stonington. When he opened to *Le Bonheur Conjugal*, out fluttered a piece of paper on which, twenty years earlier, he had typed a stanza from Byron's poem "Beppo," lines that he imagined at the time described a person he might grow to resemble:

> Then he was faithful, too, as well as amorous,
>   So that no sort of female could complain,
> Although they're now and then a little clamorous;
>   He never put the pretty souls in pain;
> His heart was one of those which most enamour us,
>   Wax to receive and marble to retain.
> He was a lover of the good old school,
> Who still become more constant as they cool.

Rather like his father, Merrill was a lover of the good old school. He'd found his own *bonheur conjugal* in 1952 with David Jackson. Jackson could play the piano, write a story, dash off a watercolor; he was ebullient, daring, funny, irresistible. Over their years together, the strains in their relationship were sometimes apparent. But they stayed together—if latterly at a certain distance from one another. It was as if Merrill were determined to keep for himself the kind of relationship his parents had thrown away. He was just as constant to his other lovers as well. He'd had affairs before he met Jackson, and several afterward. He had a way of turning each affair not only into an abiding friendship but into poetry as well. He wrote some of the most beautiful love poems of this century. He relished Borges's definition of love as the religion with a fallible god, and few poets have looked on love with such a vulnerable and wary eye:

> Where I hid my face, your touch, quick, merciful,
> Blindfolded me. A god breathed from my lips.
> If that was illusion, I wanted it to last long;
> To dwell, for its daily pittance, with us there,

Cleaning and watering, sighing with love or pain.
I hoped it would climb when it needed to the heights
Even of degradation, as I for one
Seemed, those days, to be always climbing
Into a world of wild
Flowers, feasting, tears—or was I falling, legs
Buckling, heights, depths,
Into a pool of each night's rain?
But you were everywhere beside me, masked,
As who was not, in laughter, pain, and love.

Merrill wrote openly and seriously about homosexual love long before that
was fashionable. "As in the classic account of Sarah Bernhardt descending a
spiral staircase—she stood still and *it* revolved around her—my good fortune," he wrote in his memoir, "was to stay in one place while the closet
simply disintegrated."

When I first met Merrill, he was forty-six and had earned his first full measure
of fame. *Nights and Days* had won the National Book Award, whose judges (W.
H. Auden, Howard Nemerov, and James Dickey) singled out "his insistence on
taking the kind of tough, poetic chances which make the difference between
esthetic success or failure." And he had just published *Braving the Elements*,
whose exquisite austerities mark a kind of extreme in his work. Dense and rapturous, the poems here are set amid the hazards of history and romance. His
narrative skills turn out Chekhovian vignettes like "After the Fire" or "Days of
1971," where the end of an affair helps him to a wistful self-knowledge he calls
"Proust's Law":

a) What least thing our self-love longs for most
Others instinctively withhold;
b) Only when time has slain desire
Is his wish granted to a smiling ghost
Neither harmed nor warmed, now, by the fire.

When *Braving the Elements* was awarded the 1973 Bollingen Prize, Merrill
was the subject of a *Times* editorial attacking those who continue to "reward
poetry that is literary, private, traditional." That has been a sentiment, a pecu-

liarly American fear of the Fancy, that other readers have shared. Some of his
early critics used to condescend to his work by calling it "bejewelled." Ironically,
their contempt was close to a larger truth. From the start, but nowhere more
than in this book, Merrill took his bearings from the four elements—earth, air,
fire, water—and in so many of his poems the jewel is their embodiment. Crystal
prism or emerald brooch, waterfall or geode, dragonfly or planet, whatever brilliant lens he chose, it was to inspect more carefully the natural world's wonders.
"It's not the precious," he once told a young writer, "it's the semiprecious one
has to resist." And like most strong poets, he seemed largely indifferent to his
critics. He knew his worth, and disdained the lust for celebrity. "Think what one
has to *do*," he noted wryly, "to get a mass audience. I'd rather have one perfect
reader. Why dynamite the pond in order to catch that single silver carp? Better
to find the bait that only the carp will take."

He was a poet who trusted language to tell him what anything means.
Rhyme, wordplay, paradox only help reveal the hidden wish of words.
Indeed, the OED is the collective unconscious of English speakers, he'd say;
all of our ideas and feelings are to be found there, in the endless recombina-
tions of our words. He was himself rather shy of ideas in poems. "I avert my
eyes from them," he joked, "as from the sight of a nude grandparent, not pre-
sentable, indeed taboo, until robed in images." Those images are an astonishment. He will note a hotel's "strange bed, whose recurrent dream we are,"
or describe a plot of zinnias as "pine cones in drag," or Kufic script as "all trig-
ger tail and gold vowel-sac." His lines are animated with colloquial idiom and
mercurial wit. Their perfection of tone is made to seem offhanded, their
weight of allusion and symbol is deftly balanced. If the surfaces of his poems
are sometimes difficult, it may be they only seemed so because for most of his
career other poets were loudly trumpeting the virtues of the plain style. For
his part, Merrill would say that the natural word order isn't "See Jane run."
The more *natural* way to put it is actually more complex: "Where on earth
can that child be racing off to? Why, it's little—you know, the neighbor's
brat—Jane!" So, too, the syntax of his poems darts and capers. The effect on
a reader can be vertiginous.

By the mid-1970s, his poems were growing longer. But even he was surprised
by the project that occupied him for eight years, from 1974 until 1981. Actually,
it was a project that preempted him. Since they first moved to Stonington, he

and David Jackson had, on spare evenings, sat down at a homemade Ouija board and chatted with the great dead. No sooner did he write up these encounters, in the volume *Divine Comedies* (1976), which won him the Pulitzer Prize, than the spirits demanded he attend to more rigorous lessons they would give him. "Don't you think there comes a time," Merrill explained in an interview, "when everyone, not just a poet, wants to get beyond the self? To reach, if you like, the 'god' within you? The board, in however clumsy or absurd a way, allows for precisely that. Or if it's still *yourself* that you're drawing on, then that self is much stranger and freer and more farseeing than the one you thought you knew." Resisting the impulse to be either wholly skeptical or merely credulous, Merrill sat for the lessons. The curriculum ranged from subatomic particles to cosmic forces, and the cast of thousands included Akhnaton, Pythagoras, Montezuma, T. S. Eliot, Maria Callas, bats and unicorns, scientists and neighbors, God Biology and Mother Nature. In his epic account of it all, the poet managed to make the otherwordly revelations into a very human drama of acceptance, resistance, and ambivalence. And by the time he'd gathered all seventeen thousand lines of his epic adventure into a single volume, *The Changing Light at Sandover* (1982), he had written what is—with the possible exception of Whitman's "Song of Myself"—the strangest and grandest American poem ever, at once eerie, hilarious, and heartbreaking.

His last book, *A Scattering of Salts*, is a wonderful anthology of his characteristic strengths as a poet. There are portraits and elegies, sonnets and free-verse riffs, high style and slang. There are pungent, elliptical little lyrics, and the longer, loping narratives that were his specialty. In one, he describes "family week" at a dude ranch rehab center he is visiting to be with his then lover, who has sought treatment there. The poet tries to adjust to the New Age therapies:

> . . . this wide-angle moonscape, lawns and pool,
> Patients sharing pain like fudge from home—
> As if these were the essentials,
>
> As if a month at what it invites us to think
> Is little more than a fat farm for Anorexics,
> Substance Abusers, Love & Relationship Addicts
> Could help you, light of my life, when even your shrink . . .

The message, then? That costly folderol,
Underwear made to order in Vienna,
Who needs it! Let the soul hang out
At Benetton—stone-washed, one size fits all.

It ends with a haunting, lovelorn speculation that blends the newest jargon
with one of poetry's oldest images:

And if the old patterns recur?
Ask how the co-dependent moon, another night,
Feels when the light drains wholly from her face.
Ask what that cold comfort means to her.

Cozy chats over the Ouija board acknowledge death as an event but not a fact.
They might even be said to represent at some level a denial of death. But the
three collections Merrill published during his last decade take a more realistic
look at mortality. This final book has an almost Yeatsian vigor in the face of the
end. What Merrill sees on the microscope slide is everything we dread. "Dread?
It crows for joy in the manger. / Joy? The tree sparkles on which it will die."

The earnest young poet I was in 1972 found the James Merrill who had kindly
invited me to dinner one spring night dauntingly sophisticated. His features
were faintly elfin, and his voice—a soft, cultivated baritone—drew one moth-
like toward its flickering brightness. He had read everything (I found out later
that in his twenties he had taken one winter to read all of Dickens, another for
Balzac) but skated past any ponderous discussion of literature—though he
could quote at will whole passages of Baudelaire or Da Ponte or Cole Porter.
He never played The Poet in company, but felt himself "more like a doctor at
a dinner party, just another guest until his hostess slumps to the floor or his little beeper goes off." He never read a newspaper or voted, yet was scornfully eloquent about the technocracy's myopic bureaucrats and "their sad knowledge,
their fingertip control." He worked at his desk every day, and, even to the extent
that he lived for pleasure, he lived rather simply. If he meant to be a dandy in
his dress, the results were more often merely eccentric. Old Auden wore car-
pet slippers to the opera. You could spot Merrill there in mauve Birkenstocks
over lime-green socks, neatly pressed corduroys with Navajo belt buckle, a shirt
from the Gap, a Venetian bow tie, a Loden cape and baseball cap.

His chief pleasure was friendship. Over the years, his friends ranged from Alice Toklas and Maya Deren to Richard Wilbur and Alison Lurie. To each he was tender and loyal. His friends, in turn, responded in such coin as they happened to have in their pockets. In 1968, when Stephen Yenser sent him a fervently used book—a palm-sized, velvet-covered, dog-eared copy of the *Rubaiyat* of Omar Khayam, which Merrill adored—the poet responded in kind:

> Fortunate those who back from a brief trip,
> To equinoctial storms and scholarship,
> Unwrap, first thing, a present from a friend,
> And into Omar's honeyed pages dip.

That was an inspiration, yours I mean. . . . I may ask to have the little book buried with me, in the tavern garden. The trip itself was uneventful—Atlanta, Jamaica, and long-enough in Palm Beach to get on an ill-starred plane; a motor failed, it had to limp back to Miami where it landed in a phoenix-nest of fire-trucks, its passengers by then—vacant, sun-tanned oldies all of them—more dead than alive. One of my neighbors had never flown before and decided never to do it again. The other, more worldly, simply removed her earrings and harlequin glasses against the crash landing that, with luck, we would all be able to dine out on that very evening. Life has moved at such a pace since then that perhaps after all we *did* crash and I *am* buried by the tavern with Omar in hand. I've written countless letters, finished the ballad ["The Summer People"], corrected most of an appalling English translation of a Greek friend's novel, and lost eight pounds. All very uncharacteristic behavior. Here in town [Stonington] all the cellars are flooded and everyone is agitating for McCarthy. I'm not sure what a primary is, but we're going to have one for the first time in our local history. He's clearly doomed to lose out, like all the others admired in the past by one's friends. The ballad is my pride + joy. I all but get up in the middle of the night and give it a bottle. Like an infant, it doesn't weigh very much, but its little nostrils and toenails are wonderfully complete.

Richard Howard once noted that the art of living was one of Merrill's greatest talents. "What one wants in this world," Merrill wrote. "isn't so much to 'live' as to . . . *be* lived, to be used by life for its own purposes. What has one to give but oneself?" It was always to Merrill that his friends turned when they needed advice. Here, for instance, is part of a 1973 letter he sent me from Greece. I seem then to have been in the throes of some now-forgotten crisis of the heart. How sweetly he edged up to my worries, and even more sweetly moved past them. He began by describing the crowded summer in Athens, and his being content to stay blithely above it. Then he expands from details to his theme:

The iron gates of life have seldom seen such traffic, to judge from the confused rumor that reaches us here in the shade of the pearly ones. The real absurdity, you will say (and I'll agree, it's all so novel), is to feel in one's bones how utterly a boundary has been crossed. Here one is in Later Life, and it's perfectly pleasant really, not for a moment that garden of cactus and sour grapes I'd always assumed it *must* be. Oh dear, this sort of thing is probably just what you mean by my being "recessed" into myself. But it's odd. I mean, the times of greatest recession into the self have always been, for me, times of helpless suffering, such as you're going through; when there's no escape from the self. Perhaps any circumstance, any frame of mind, content, pain, trust, distrust, is a niche that limits visibility —for both the occupant and the onlooker? I read your last letter, in any case, with pangs of recognition. There's no special comfort, is there? in being understood at times like these. One is mortified by one's predicament, and at the same moment so curiously proud of its ramifications. You won't be ready yet to *like* the fact of belonging to a very large group who've all had—allowing for particular differences— the same general experience. Later on, when your sense of humor and proportion returns, that fact ought rather to please you: to have so shared in the—or at least *a*—human condition.

The other evening we made an exception and went next door to meet Alan Ansen's houseguest, a Mr Burroughs—a sallow, nondescript party who talked of nothing but drugs and sex-crimes, just like my mother's Atlanta friends. Luckily dear Tony [his Alexandrian friend, Tony Parigory] was there, and told us another of his Egyptian stories. Onto a Cairo bus one hot summer day, when "everyone" has fled town, climbs a man holding a huge watermelon in both arms. Unable to support himself, he lurches against various passengers one of whom flares up. There are words. The man with the watermelon draws himself up: "Hm! It's obvious you don't know who I am." The other looks him over, then slowly ticks off each point on his fingers: "August. In Cairo. On a bus. Holding a watermelon. Who could you be?"

If it helps to write me about your troubles, don't let shyness hold you back. And if you'd rather I didn't comment, another time, upon what you tell me, I should understand that very well.

Of course, he gave a great deal more than advice to his friends. He was a soft touch, and had learned the difficult art of giving money away gracefully. A friend's staggering medical bill or the downpayment on a house, appeals from ballet companies or animal shelters, stories of neglected old poets on the skids or a young painter who needed equipment . . . his sympathy was easily sparked. In the late 1950s, dismayed by the size of his inheritance, he used a good chunk of it to establish the Ingram Merrill Foundation, whose board of directors was empowered to award grants to writers and artists. Over the years, hundreds of people were helped. The edge was always given to the promising beginner.

What Merrill couldn't give away was the stigma that came with his wealth and privilege. Epicurus famously said that riches don't alleviate, only change one's troubles. The fortune that gave Merrill the chance both to distance himself from the family who made it and to pursue an odd, intricate career was, I'd guess, a nagging source of embarrassment for him and may have occasioned, in turn, his aversion to grand hotels and restaurants, his recycled razor blades and spartan diet. He used long ago to confuse his companions by declaring, "Thank goodness I come from poor parents." He meant that his parents' values had been formed—by the example of their hard-working, middle-class parents—before they had money. In a sense, his own values were old-fashioned. What sustained Merrill was a dedication to his calling, a high ambition, and a deeply moral purpose. If we give equal weight to each word, then this definition of a poet he once offered sums him up: he was "a man choosing the words he lives by."

When Merrill's ashes were sent back to be buried in Stonington, a box of papers came too. Among them was a poem called "Koi." Behind the house he had been renting in Tucson for the winter is a small ornamental pool of koi, the Japanese carp. The poem—the last he wrote, a couple of weeks before he died—is about those fish and his little Jack Russell terrier, Cosmo. Of course it wasn't written *as* a last poem, but circumstances give it a special poignancy.

Also sent home was his notebook. It's open now on my desk. He'd kept a series of notebooks over the years, their entries irregular, often fragmentary. Things overheard or undergone. Dreams, lists, lines. An image or anagram. The writing—even the handwriting—is swift and elegant. But the last page of this notebook is nearly indecipherable. Suddenly, at the end, you can *see* the difficulty he was having: the script is blurred, and that may be because he had lost his glasses. His breathing too was labored. On Saturday, he'd been admitted to the hospital with a bout of acute pancreatitis. I spoke with him by telephone on Sunday, the night before he died, and asked about his breathing. He struggled to say that, though he'd been given oxygen, the doctors were unconcerned and had scheduled his release. The rest of the conversation was banter and gossip and plans for the future: a cataract operation, the new *Pelléas* at the Met. His notebook, though, tells another, more anxious story. The last page is dated 5.ii.95, the day before his death. There are two dozen lines, sketches for a poem to be titled "The Next to Last Scene." Typically it starts by looking around his hospital room, and opens with what in retrospect seems a heart-catching line: "A room with every last convenience." It glances at TV set, cassette player, smiling lover. He would often, when drafting a poem, fill out the end of a line, knowing where he wanted to go although not exactly how he would get there. He'd done so here. I can make out "To see the other through." And then, the very last thing he wrote, "To set the other free."

To set the other free. Who is this "other"? The longer I gaze at the page, the more resonant the phrase becomes. Is it everything beyond and beloved by the self: the man in his life, the world's abundance? Or all that burdens the soul, distracts the heart? The psyche? The imagination? Or perhaps he means—this has been the case for the last fifty years—the enthralled reader. It is still intolerable to think that there will be no more of his resplendent, plangent, wise poems, that their author is like the mirror ceremonially broken at the end of *Sandover*, "giving up its whole / Lifetime of images."

19 . M A S T E R S

?

?

?

?

?

?

?

?

?

?

?

?

?

?

?

?

?

?

?

?

"No art is less spontaneous than mine," wrote Degas. "What I do is the result of reflection, of the study of the masters."

Few artists have been so rigorous in their homage to the past. Though his fame in part rests on his realism, on his reputation as a witness to the underside of contemporary life—backstage, brothel, sweatshop—it was a *studied* view. From his notebook: "Ah! Giotto! let me see Paris, and you, Paris, let me *see* Giotto!" Scenes from daily life, in fact, were illustrations of lessons learned from paintings—or rather, the means taken to understand those lessons, to approximate those perfections.

As soon as he left school at eighteen—the redoubtable Lycée Louis-le-Grand from which Baudelaire had earlier been expelled and where Degas himself was an indifferent student with a fondness for the classics—he registered as a copyist both at the Louvre and at the Cabinet des Estampes of the Bibliothèque Nationale. He preferred fifteenth- and sixteenth-century Italian pictures. "I copied all the Primitives in the Louvre," he boasted. Three years later, during his apprenticeship in Italy, he copied obsessively. Accompanying Gustave

Moreau, he copied in the Villa Farnesina, in the Sistine Chapel, in the Villa Medici, in the Doria Pamphili and the Borghese and the Capitoline. He copied Claude and Sodoma, Correggio and Raphael, Veronese and Giulio Romano. He copied in the Uffizi; he copied the Signorellis in Orvieto; in Venice, Carpaccio and Giorgione; in Pisa, the Benozzo Gozzoli frescoes in the Campo Santo. That is why, after all, a painter went to Italy, for his "reunion with antiquity." The storied light there emanated from marble and varnish.

But, unlike others, Degas went on copying in Paris well into his thirties, and for his own purposes. His 1861 copy of Mantegna's *Crucifixion*, for instance, is not simply a reproduction; it is, instead, an effort to study the master's "spirit and love," but combine them with "the verve and color of Veronese." All facility has been abjured: details are deleted, and figures blurred, the better to concentrate on the picture's composition. He copied works of ancient art from Assyria and Egypt as well as from Greece and Rome. He also copied "modern" art: David, Ingres, Daumier (an especial favorite), Whistler, Meissonier, and others. As late as 1897, when he was sixty-five, he was still copying paintings by Delacroix and Mantegna. "The masters must be copied over and over again," he scolded, "and it is only after proving yourself a good copyist that you should reasonably be permitted to draw a radish from nature." Not that he ever approved of the outdoors, province of the Impressionists: "If I were the government, I would have a squad of gendarmes to keep an eye on these people painting landscapes from nature. Oh! I do not wish anyone dead; I would, however, agree to spraying them with a little bird shot, for starters!" Art is indoors, and the scene of instruction remains its subject. The enclosures of canvas and frame inform every decision; the walls and floors in his paintings are metaphysical perspectives and emotional boundaries. In 1855, at the age of twenty-three, he was already making sketches of actresses at the theater—in this case, of the tragedienne Adelaide Ristori in Schiller's *Mary Stuart* during its first Paris performance. All his life he loved stages, and not just at the Opéra. The woman at her toilette, or in the *modiste's* shop, pictures by Claude or Poussin, his genre and history paintings, the arrangement of sitters in his photographs—all these are sets as well. Of his outdoor scenes, perhaps the ritual of the horse race may be considered an enclosure no less than the track or paddock. Because of his self-conscious regard for tradition, everything is copied *into* a confinement, and reproduces the act of viewing.

One day in 1862 at the Louvre, while copying Velázquez's *Infanta Margarita*, he met Manet, who interrupted him because he was fascinated to notice Degas copying directly onto a copper plate. There began a lifelong friendship. Some years earlier, having gone to his school friend Valpinçon's house to copy Ingres's voluptuary *Bather*, which the family owned—her white expanse of back would figure in so many of Degas's own bathers later on—he was told by the elder Valpinçon that Ingres himself was there the day before to ask for the picture, and had been refused. The young Degas was incensed by "an affront like that to a man like Monsieur Ingres," his idol. Thus persuaded to relent and lend the picture, Valpinçon took Degas with him the next day to Ingres's studio. Seeing his guests to the door on their way out, the old master suffered a dizzy spell and slumped to the floor. Degas rushed to help, and for years afterward would tell people, "I once held Ingres in my arms."

But, of course, the point is that he had long since put himself into *their* hands, the masters'—and quite literally. In his very first *Self-Portrait*, of 1855, he portrays himself with a draftsman's charcoal holder in hand, as if just looking up from a drawing class at the École des Beaux-Arts. When he copied from life, his figures assume attitudes in art. And when he copied pictures, he often tried not just to reproduce the object but to recreate the process by which it came to be. So his 1860 pen-and-wash drawing of the figural outlines and harmonic contrasts of light and shade in Poussin's *The Triumph of Flora* seems to mimic a supposed preliminary drawing Poussin himself might have made. (The gesture also confirms Degas's famous axiom: "Drawing is not the same as form, it is a way of seeing form.") In 1859, his *Portrait of a Young Woman* takes Leonardo's red chalk drawing in the Uffizi and renders it, "completes" it, in oil. In both cases, Degas's desire to *become* the master, to deconstruct or extend the sacred intentions, results from his profound sense—a very nineteenth-century sense—that art has a double nature, as both mystery and problem. On the one hand, it is a set of secrets to be marvelled at and plumbed. The acolyte in him, noted Paul Valéry, attended on "feelings whose great bitterness and exaltation were nourished by his subtle appreciation of the masters, his longing to possess the secret knowledge he credited them with, and his continual awareness of their mutually exclusive perfections." On the other hand, art is a science, a set of variables and conditions that can be studied or manipulated to serve a higher intention. This is the side of Degas that studied Eadweard Muybridge's photographic sequences of running horses, or mimicked a dancer's positions or the fussy way a woman took her tram seat—his attentions so precise as nearly to have become those women.

It is on this axis that he sought to reconcile his study and his practice, his techniques and his motifs, Giotto and Paris.

It is this same conviction that his critics see in the cold precisions of his pictures and in the elusive melancholy of his sitters, their heads so often turned away, sulking or brooding or distracted. Here is the heart of the solitude, the isolation, that is his characteristic subject: this inward turning. The self-absorption of his dancers and *chanteuses*, his whores and ironing or bathing women, is apparent. They are types of *concentration*, some interiorized idea they have embodied and are trying to express. Degas doesn't presume to explain their moods or reveal their minds, only to portray how little regard they have for the spectator. Desiré Dihau, intent on his bassoon, in *The Orchestra of the Opéra* (1870). Mme Paul Valpinçon staring quizzically out of the frame, away from both the overwhelming motif of the picture and its source outside, the garden just visible through the open window behind her, in *Woman Leaning near a Vase of Flowers* (1865). The heavily veiled faces of the two women conversing in *At the Races* (1877). And more obvious choices: the slumped hopelessness, two pairs of eyes distinctly looking nowhere at all, in *The Absinthe Drinker* (1876). Or the couple in *Interior* (1869), guilt obscuring her eyes altogether though the lamp seems to look through her desperation, and through his gutted propriety. Or *The Bellelli Family* (1867), each consciously avoiding the other's look, austere, dark shapes against the richly ornamented bourgeois background. In so many pictures, Degas's subjects seem as remote as the masters seemed to him, and as intimate. I sometimes think he sought kindred souls as his sitters, correspondences. Though his model Pauline reported that in later life he would sing arias from Italian operas to her as he worked, explain the texts, and mutter "Delightful, no?" and sometimes even lead her down from her pose to dance as he hummed, for the most part he was drawn to silence: the mute poetry of model or masterpiece. In one of his sonnets, Degas speaks of the language of the ballet, "le mystère / Des mouvements d'un corps éloquent et sans bruit." And he links this with a "Tradition sereine, impénétrable aux fous." These are the words of a painter who has spent a lifetime looking at pictured bodies.

Degas wrote twenty sonnets. There are other, occasional verses scattered among his notebooks. On one page of verse are notes that refer to this passage from Saint-Évremond:

Fortunate would be the soul that could completely reject certain passions and could merely anticipate certain others. It would be without fear, without sadness, without hatred, without jealousy. It would desire without eagerness, hope without worry, and enjoy without transport.

A sonnet too can reject and anticipate certain passions. That may be what attracted Degas to the form. In an 1889 letter to Berthe Morisot, Mallarmé reported on Degas's literary enthusiasm: "His own poetry is distracting him, for—and this will be the notable event of the winter—he is now into his fourth sonnet. In fact, he is no longer of this world, or is perturbed by the constraints of a new art, in which, upon my word, he conducts himself very prettily." He went about writing sonnets in much the same way he went about painting. He bought a volume of Ronsard's sonnets to study, along with a copy of Théodore de Banville's *Petit traité de versification française* and a rhyming dictionary. The results are respectably Parnassian. It is interesting to take note of the frequent mythological allusions in these poems. Whatever his present subject, it is usually drawn into a classical perspective; even a sonnet to Mary Cassatt's parrot ends with an invocation of the "mares de Cythère." No doubt he counted on the classicizing effect of the sonnet form itself, of those ways by which it maneuvers material into submitting to tradition's conventional wisdoms. In one sonnet, addressed to the sonneteer Heredia, he takes up the matter with a sly irony:

Inoubliable outil de dure poésie
Que vous pouvez, poète, à la forge d'un dieu
Marteler, ciseler et rougir dans le feu,
Pour que sa griffe fume en la rime choisie.

Suez, avec le poids d'une armure de fer,
A suivre en ses détours une femme cachée
Qui tremble moins que vous.

Degas's description here functions as a history of the sonnet—than which, says Valéry, no literary discipline creates more tension between will and inclination, intention and finished work, or more compels the mind to accept form and content as being of equal importance. And the poetic figuration here may stand in as well for Degas's own pursuit of his model, her silent body: the copyist in front of *La Peinture*.

To prolong one's contemplation of any art only heightens one's awareness of insoluble dilemmas of choice. The counterclaims of tradition and contingency trouble both painter and poet, and it is impossible not to suppose that Degas was drawn to the sonnet as he had been drawn to the sixteenth-century Italian masters. His relationship to these fixed, though by no means static, traditions cannot be mistaken for academicism, however petulant his insistence (as he puts it in a letter) that "art does not reach out, it sums up." The proper understanding is Andrew Forge's, in his magisterial study of Degas: "Again and again, aspects of his work present themselves as a transformation of some aspect of the tradition, an aspect that is so deeply understood that he is able to dismantle it, split it from its context, and, in reconstructing it, infuse it with meaning and freshness." After all, it was Degas who said, in response to a woman who asked why he painted ballet dancers so often, "Because it is all that is left us of the combined movement of the Greeks." Who had thought to prop his pictures next to frieze or calyx, as they were in his own mind? The *limbs* of these women, their stylized gestures of extension, fascinate him, as later, in his series of bathers, a sculptural interest in the torso dominates the pictures.

In one of his notebooks, Degas wrote these directions to himself: "Finally, study from every perspective a figure or an object, no matter what. Use a mirror for this—without moving from your place. Only the place would be raised or lowered, you would circle round it." Once again, this notion, this combination, of study and reflection. Having allowed the masters to be the mirrors for his own intentions, it is not surprising that he so often included mirrors in his pictures. They may serve as emblems of conscience, as they do in *The Bellelli Family* or in *Interior*, where the mirror stands between and behind the guilty lovers and picks up the light they have turned from. Or they may be emblems of solitude, as they are when his women practice or make up or dress themselves before one. It is also a way for the painter to contemplate his subject from another angle, of course, but from the start Degas was fascinated by reflection and doubleness. Only consider his early drawing *Two Studies of the Head of a Man* (1857). Though it's never mentioned, the angle of the heads suggests the man is standing next to a mirror. (Compare it with the 1875 portrait, *Mme Jeantaud Before a Mirror*.) Later in his career, water served to create the angles of reflection. It is there, of course, as early as *Mlle Fiocre in the Ballet "La Source"* (1868). But I am thinking particularly of his series of bathers. In her shallow, mirror-round tubs you can see both the woman's reflection and her shadow. In two pictures from 1886, both called *The Tub*, the woman is crouching or bent over, sponging herself, each like a dancer in a *position*, the mass of her white flesh held up for us to look in for ourselves.

In the work of his old age, a time when abstraction and intense colors enter his paintings, he turned more assiduously to photography, preferring—as always—indoor shots that he himself would develop, enlarge, and retouch. Perhaps his most famous is a portrait of Renoir and Mallarmé, taken one long evening in 1895 before nine oil lamps. Renoir is seated, his head cocked warily back, studying us. The poet is standing beside him, hands in his coat pockets, looking pensively and in noble profile down on the painter. A large mirror dominates the background. Mallarmé's wife and their daughter Geneviève can just be seen on a sofa against the opposing panelled wall—"like phantoms," said Valéry . And next to them, Degas himself and his camera. But the light necessary to take the picture has effaced the artist in its aura. At the center of the picture, then, is an emptiness—not unlike the small blind spot that Degas early on developed in the middle of his line of vision. Masters and mirrors are means for looking at the world, not at the self.

Forty years before this scene was set, Ingres had given some advice (so Valéry reports the anecdote) to the young painter who had held him after his fall. "Young man," he told Degas, "never work from nature. Always from memory, or from the engravings of the masters." Ingres also knew that "ideal" beauty derives from distortion, from altering the relation of parts—as memory does. Degas never copied, he *worked* from memory, worked to find in his subject its memory of an ideal. Those who look for big blockbuster pictures in Degas's oeuvre are—once they've praised *The Bellelli Family*—disappointed. But they've missed the point of his method. The "big" pictures are those alluded to in his own smaller renderings of their spirit and techniques.

Valéry also reported that "Degas liked talking about painting, but could ill bear anyone else doing so. From writers he would not suffer it at all. He made it his business to silence them."

?
?
?
?
?
?
?
?
?
?
?

a translation of Quintus Horatius Flaccus,
Ep. II.iii, known as the Ars Poetica
for Stephen Yenser

?
?
?
?
?
?
?
?
?
?
?

Like one of those noble statues in the corridors of the Vatican Museum, for
centuries considered an epitome of the art but today often hurried by, the *Ars
Poetica* was a standard of taste from the Renaissance to the Romantic Age. It
was a hornbook for European classicism, a source of proverbial wisdom, the
folklore of the literary imagination. It is impossible to read Petrarch or Pope,
Johnson or Byron, Montaigne or Rousseau, Du Bellay or Hölderlin, and not
think of Horace's influence. But since the Romantics, the ambitions of our
poets have changed, and Horace's poem is now more often studied as a
curiosity than read as a model. Neither sort of reading, however, captures the
poem's force. It remains a discursive guide, of course, though one whose
practical advice the expert is more likely to confirm than the beginner to follow. But as a poem in its own right, with its ingenious tropes and shifts of
tone, the *Ars Poetica* shimmers with what Petronius once praised as Horace's
curiosa felicitas, and at the same time is shot through with the *furchtbare
Realität* that Goethe discerned in even the most sumptuous of Horace's
odes.

Quintus Horatius Flaccus was born in Apulia on December 8, 65 B.C. His devoted father, a freed slave who worked as an auctioneer's agent and had a small unprofitable farm, was determined that Horace be given the best possible education. He took the boy to Rome where he was sent to the finest schools—his stern tutor Orbilius applied the cane and drilled the boy in Homer—and later to advanced studies in Athens. While in Greece, Horace joined the cause of the exiled Brutus and enlisted as a military tribune in the doomed republican army. He fought at Philippi and later wrote of himself as if he were a character in Homer: that, trembling in the great battle, he had been rescued by Mercury, who wrapped him in a mist. By 41 B.C., following Octavian's general amnesty, Horace had returned to Rome, secured a position as a scribe in the civil service, and begun a literary career. In 39, his friends Vergil and Varius introduced him to Maecenas, who eventually championed the poet and provided him both an allowance and a Sabine farm—where, short, stout, and prematurely gray, Horace liked to sit in the sun and meditate on the distracting follies of the capital and the calm delights of the countryside. His *Satires* and *Epodes*, in which he set about adapting and polishing rude models, won him fame and declared his Roman Alexandrianism, his preference for an urbane, lapidary ingenuity. The first three books of his *Odes*, which naturalized for Latin poetry the spirit of the Greek lyric, attracted the emperor's favor. Horace, who admired Augustus but maintained his independence from the accustomed imperial flatteries, declined the emperor's request to become his private secretary, but not his insistence on a new book of *Odes* or his request to compose the *Carmen Saeculare*, the Centennial Hymn for the great public celebration in 17 B.C. of the secular games meant to commemorate five centuries of Roman power. The twenty-three *Epistles* written toward the end of his life contemplate the golden mean with the graceful wit of a sensible hedonist, a superstitious *raisonneur*. As verse letters, their tone is intimate, dominated by his personality's genial sophistication rather than by the strictures of any philosophy. In these poems above all, as Pope said, "*Horace* still charms with graceful Negligence, / And without Method *talks* us into Sense." The poet died on November 27, 8 B.C. Suetonius tells us that Horace's last thoughts were of his most faithful readers: on his deathbed, too weak to sign his will, he asked that his estate be given to Augustus and his body be buried near that of Maecenas, who had died a few months earlier.

It is thought that the *Ars Poetica* (first given that title by Quintilian, three generations after the poet's death) was written in 10 B.C. and was Horace's last
poem; perhaps for that reason it is also considered his last word on the subject
of his art. But the poetic qualities he praises here had been singled out—or better, exemplified—in all of his earlier work. In fact, like most criticism by poets,
the *Ars Poetica* casually elevates personal preferences into universal principles.
Its axioms and opinions derive from his career as both lyric poet and satirist.
The two impulses are balanced in his account. As before, the traditionalist in
Horace turns to the Greeks. Greek literature, it might be said, was his home-
land: a familiar, beloved landscape. From the Greeks he had learned that
power resides in discipline, that a sophisticated technique alone possesses the
subtle buoyancy to rise above the ordinary, and that wisdom, rather than
finesse or sincerity or bluster, is finally the true source of poetic strength.
Above all, from the Greeks he learned the value of decorum, which is to be
understood not as restraint but as symmetry, not as a rigid unity but as the harmony of details. Likewise, the satirist in Horace favored good sense. If he urged
a poetry of limits and measure, it was because he viewed the writing of poetry
as a moral responsibility. He makes memory itself a moral principle; his rural
origins, his Greek studies, his instinct for loyalty and tradition—he grounds his
work first of all in his sense of the past. If he admits Homer has faults, he most
admires the old poet's spirit and cherishes him because he is not just an artist
but a teacher. And what the best poets have to teach us has to do as much with
life as with art: the balance between artifice and nature, between technique
and inspiration, between gravity and play.

It may seem odd that a poem praising classical design, and insisting on proportion and unity, should itself resemble a hodgepodge. Coleridge called the
poem an "unmethodical miscellany." But that is part of its point, or at least of
its fiction. The tone and drift of the poem derive from its being a verse letter.
Personality rather than philosophy dominates. It is not a treatise, like Aristotle's.
The poem poses as a letter to Piso and his two sons, the elder of whom seems
to want to write a play. (Porphyrion claimed it is addressed to Lucius
Calpurnius Piso Frugi, the pontifex, a consul in 15 B.C. But that is disputed and
nothing is certain about these Pisos—which quite properly shifts our attention
to the speaker and his sly methods.) But the broad movements of the poem are
clear: his discussion of poetry in general, his consideration of the dramatic
poem, and finally his analysis of the character of the poet. His preoccupation

with drama should remind us of his concern for the expressive and moral grandeur that different poetic genres—the epic, the lyric, the drama—may aspire to. Horace's estimate of the poet and his task, whichever form that task assumes, is a shrewd one. The *Ars Poetica* opens with a grotesque account of a muddled poem, and closes with a scornful account of a befuddled poet—as if one might turn into the monstrosity he imagines.

There have been English versions of Horace's poem, or parts of it, from Chaucer on. Queen Elizabeth I—at the age of sixty-five and in spite of her failing eyesight (which probably accounts for some missing lines; her vanity forced her to forgo the use of spectacles)—translated the first 178 lines. Her version opens this way:

If to a mans hed a panter wold
  A horsis neck conjoine
And coulored fethers ad therto
  With limmes togither set,
That face aboue of woman faire,
  The rest fowle like the moudy fische;
For suche a hap, my frindz,
  Could you your laughtar kipe?

The bouncy tetrameters of Christopher Smart's 1767 translation have a certain slapdash appeal, but none of the Latin poet's subtlety:

A poem cannot be compleat,
Tho' beautiful, if 'tis not sweet,
Till by its pathos it can seize
The soul, and bear her where it please.
  Expressive or of joy or pain,
As human aspects smile again
Upon the smilers, so their eyes
Will with the tearful sympathise.
If you wou'd have me really weep,
Your own distresses must be deep.

Byron calls his 1811 "Hints from Horace" an allusion to the *Ars Poetica*. It is part translation, part pastiche, and done with an easy, loping wit:

'T is not enough, ye bards, with all your art,
To polish poems; they must touch the heart:
Where'er the scene be laid, whate'er the song,
Still let it bear the hearer's soul along;
Command your audience or to smile or weep,
Whiche'er may please you—anything but sleep.
The poet claims our tears; but, by his leave,
Before I shed them, let me see *him* grieve.

Contemporary translations, for the most part, seem either versified pen-
dantry that would make Gilbert Murray blush or idle updatings in the manner
of Ezra Pound. Nothing dates faster than relevance, and I see no need for this
Art of Poetry to condescend to readers by assuming they are uninterested in
Horace's own range of references. (There are a few appended notes for those
who may wish to plump their classroom memories.) At the same time, I have
wanted a metrical and slightly formal line to keep the *poem* foremost. If we
allow the congenial voice to lull us into forgetting that this is also a remarkable
verbal performance, we underestimate Horace's achievement. It was Pope
who said that Horace *"judg'd* with *Coolness* tho' he sung with *Fire."* I have tried
to let the brilliance gleam through the elegance and would be "Content, if
hence th' Unlearn'd their Wants may view, / The Learn'd reflect on what
before they knew."

•

Suppose the painter chose to join a human
Head to a horse's neck, and then lay motley
Feathers over odd-lot limbs, so the graceful
Woman above gave way below to a loathsome
Slimy fish—one look, no? and you'd be
Laughing, friends. Believe me, my dear Pisos,
Pictures like that recall the book whose idle
Fancies are framed like a sick man's dreams,
So any shape might be thought either head or foot.
"A certain boldness is always allowed, to painters
And poets alike." True: we claim this indulgence

And grant it. But not to pair the wild and tame,
Not mate the birds with serpents, tigers with lambs.
   A purple patch or two may glitter on a poem's
Grave beginnings and great promise, some sequin
Like "the grove and altar of Diana"
Or "streams that scamper on through fairest fields."
The rapid Rhine, say, or a rainbow is described.
They have their place . . . but here? Perhaps you're skilled
At drawing cypresses: what help if you
Must paint a sailor leaping from a wreck?
A wine jar's begun: why does the potter's wheel
Turn out a water jug? Whatever it is
At last you make, only let it be consistent.
   Most every poet, good sir and worthy sons,
Deceives himself by a sort of truth. I struggle
For concision, and grow obscure. You're after polish,
But lack nerve and fire. The grand gesture sputters.
The cautious, who fear the tempest, merely creep.
Others, to adorn monotony, depict
A dolphin in the woods, a boar in the waves.
Without true art, avoiding faults is error.
In a shop nearby the gladiators' school,
A craftsman in bronze can cast fingernails
And copy curly hair, but since he slights
A plan for the whole, his parts have no effect.
With a work in mind, I'd no more want to be
That man than, praised for my dark hair and darker
Eyes, still face the world with a crooked nose.
   Writers must match their subjects to their strengths,
And weigh what they can bear or should shrug off.
Neither eloquence nor clarity deserts
The writer who chooses his theme to suit his powers.
What gives value and charm to order, if I'm right,
Is this: to say now what ought to be said now
And postpone the rest, neglect it for the moment.
For his promised poem, an author must be prepared

To embrace one phrase and yet despise another.
   Also, be wary of fabricating words:
He speaks best who makes the known word new
By clever combinations. And if by chance
You must use novel terms for knotty points,
You can coin such words as codgers never heard.
Leave will be given, when taken in moderation,
And new-minted words gain prompter currency
If frugally forged from ore that's mined in Greece.
Why grant to Plautus or Caecilius a freedom
Refused to Varius and Vergil? And who'd begrudge
Me my few, when the tongues of Cato and Ennius
Have enriched the native style and called old things
By new names? It is, as it has always been,
Permitted to issue words imprinted with
The present. As forests shed their leaves each year—
The earliest dropping first—so old words die
And newborn ones will bloom and flourish next.
All we own we owe to death. Lord Neptune
In his temple may save our fleet from northern gales
(A princely deed); or barren marshes only
Oars could ply now feel the heavy plow
And feed the neighboring towns; or a river shift
Its ruinous course, be taught to mend its way—
No matter. Mortal projects come to grief.
The fame and glories of a style will fade.
Banished words will be restored, and many
Now in fashion fall, as standards change.
Usage makes the rules and rights of speech.
   Homer made hexameters give voice
To kings and captains, the gloomy feats of war.
Grief was first expressed in jagged lines,
And then our gratitude for answered prayers,
Though scholars still dispute who first composed
The elegy: that case remains in court.
Fury armed Archilochus with his iamb,

A foot either comic sock and tragic buskin
Fits, well-suited both to dialogue
And silencing or stirring up the crowd.
To lyric verse the Muse assigned the gods
And all their kind, the champion fighter, the horse
Who wins the prize, the lover's woes or wine's
Abandon. Should I fail to note the shapes
And tones of different forms, why call me poet?
Would I prefer from false pride to be ignorant
Or to learn? A comic theme will never work
In tragic meters, nor can Thyestes' feast
Be told in strains that comic authors use
For low life. Let each style keep its place.
Even comedy may raise its voice,
When angry Chremes swells and shakes his fist;
So too in tragedy poor Telephus
Or outcast Peleus may often weep
In prose—to catch the audience by its heart
The hero puts aside the bluff and bombast.
　　　It's not enough that poems be exquisite.
Let empathy prevail and lead the listener's
Heart. A face will smile to see a smile,
Or weep at tears. If you would have me grieve,
Then first feel grief yourself. It's then the hero's
Woes will sting me; if the lines are ill-sorted
I snigger or yawn. Melancholy becomes
The sad face, a threat the angry look;
Banter suits the grin, gravity the frown.
For Nature has fashioned us for every fortune:
She gladdens or infuriates us, drags us down
To earth and crushes us beneath our sorrows,
Then lets the tongue tell the soul's story.
If the speaker's phrase and fortune are at odds,
Patrons and standees both will roar with laughter.
God or hero—who speaks makes all the difference—
The mellow old man or the hot-blooded youth,

The matron in her prime or bustling nurse,
The travelling merchant or tiller of the soil,
From savage Colchis or soft Assyria,
From headstrong Thebes or law-abiding Argos.
     Either follow tradition or else invent
Something coherent. If you should decide
To bring back, say, illustrious Achilles,
Make him zealous, wrathful, ruthless, wild,
Arrogant of the law and quick to the sword.
Let Medea be savage, unmoved, let Ino weep,
Ixion betray, Io roam, Orestes lament.
If to stage an untried scene you dare portray
A brand-new character, keep him the same
Beginning to end, entirely of a piece.
     It's hard to make original what's common.
But better divide the old tale of Troy by acts
Than be the first to try a theme unsung
Or overlooked. To make the public domain
Your own, don't dawdle on the beaten path
Or slavishly copy a story word for word
Or imitate so narrowly you're trapped
Either by shame or by a line of thought.
And don't begin like the ancient cyclic poets:
"Of Priam's fate and glorious wars I sing."
What follows such a feebleminded line?
Mountains will labor to bring forth a mouse.
Better the poet who starts off sensibly:
"Tell me, Muse, of him who saw the world
And ways of men after the fall of Troy."
There's not just smoke, but fire to flicker on
The wondrous tales—of Scylla and Charybdis,
The Cyclops and Lotus-eaters. He doesn't wind
The story of Diomedes all the way back
To the death of Meleager, nor the Trojan war
To Leda's egg. He races to the crisis,
Starts in the middle of things, as if we know

It all, and what he cannot bring to light
He leaves behind. He blends so craftily
The facts with fiction that his poem's seamless,
First line to last, midpoint on to the end.

     Listen now: here's what your public and I
Both expect. If you want an audience
To stay for the final curtain and then to cheer
When the singer says "Applaud," you must depict
Those traits each age of man brings out, and give
To their different years and natures the proper tone.
The child who's learned at last to speak and walk
Enjoys his playmates best; his tantrums flare
And are forgotten as the hours change.
The beardless youth, his tutor out of sight,
Loves dogs and horses, the open sunny fields;
He's wax for vice to mold, contemptuous
Of good advice, a grasshopper, a spendthrift,
Quick to desire and quick to change his mind.
With altered aims, the grown man's temperament
Seeks wealth and friends, is slavish to position,
Wary to do what soon must be undone.
Misfortunes swarm about the old man's head
Either because he's greedy but a miser
Afraid to open his purse, or because in all
He does he dithers, deferring hopes yet grasping
For a future, surly, peevish, given to praise
The days of his youth while censuring the young.
The advancing years lend a happiness
We pay in turn to time. So lest we mistake
The parts—give old to young or man to boy—
We must align the age with its attributes.

     Events are either acted or described.
More readily than to what is heard the mind
Responds to what is seen, what the spectator
Beholds. And yet it's best to keep offstage
What oughtn't to be shown; what can be quickly

Recounted need not then be dramatized.
Medea shouldn't butcher her boys in public,
Nor vengeful Atreus cook up a human stew,
Nor Procne turn into a nightingale,
Cadmus into a snake. When forced to look
At such stuff, I'm incredulous and put out.

  Any play that wants a subsequent performance
Must have five acts—neither more nor fewer.
Be sure no god is allowed to intervene
Unless none but he can solve the tangled plot;
And don't introduce a fourth speaking part.

  The chorus should take a player's crucial role,
Not merely sing between the acts in ways
That don't advance or even fit the action.
It should favor sense and offer sound advice,
Curb the angry and hearten the high-minded.
Let it praise plain living and prudent laws,
The justice and peace that come through open gates.
Let it keep its secrets but beseech the gods
That fortune bless the stricken, elude the proud.

  The flute—not as nowadays the trumpet's brazen
Rival but a reed with simple stops—
At one time tuned up and accompanied the chorus.
Its music filled the not yet crowded theater
Where people gathered, few enough to count,
Modest people, frugal and chaste in their ways.
But when they colonized new territories,
When thicker walls encircled their cities and wine
Freely flowed by day to celebrate
A festival, the times grew lax, and the tunes.
What taste can you expect from know-nothings,
Those bumpkins seated next to decent townsmen?
And so to his primitive art the flute-player
Added speed and display, strutting across the stage
Fluttering his robe. To the simple lyre as well
New strings were fitted, and daring mannerisms

Produced a singular eloquence. Ideas
And prophecies then grew as riddling as Delphi.
   The tragic poet, the first who sang to compete
For a scrawny goat, soon stripped his shaggy satyrs—
Dignified amid the fooling—as if the lure
Of novelty alone could hold a crowd
Drunk and unruly after the sacred rites.
To get away with laughing, mocking satyrs,
To jump from grave to gay, have no god or hero
Hold the stage in royal gold or purple
Only to reappear in a dreary shed.
And to avoid the filth, must he grab at clouds?
Tragedy, disdaining comic babble,
Will blush to join the satyrs' wantonness,
Like a matron asked to dance on holidays.
Were I to write a satyr play, good Pisos,
I wouldn't use the plainest words alone
Nor strain to deny myself the tragic note.
So what if Davus jokes with Pythias,
Who's cheated poor Simo, or with Silenus,
The young god's guide and tutor? I mean to make
My poems from familiar things so anyone
Can match me—and sweat and struggle as he tries:
Such is the power of order and artfulness,
Such the glories attending the commonplace.
When a satyr's led on from the woods, I think,
He shouldn't talk like a know-it-all or play
The lecherous dandy or flaunt his bawdy gags.
The high-born and well-off will likely take offense;
They never will approve, much less applaud,
What the roasted-nut-crunching crowd may cheer.
   Two syllables—one short, one long—are called
An iamb, a nimble foot that stamped the name
Of trimeter upon a line, though six
Beats, the same throughout, are sounded. Not long
Ago, to reach the ear more weightily,

It adopted slow spondees into the family,
Obliging and patient but keeping for itself
The second and fourth positions. This iamb seldom
Appears in the famous trimeters of Accius,
Or in Ennius who lugged his ponderous lines
Onto the stage, open to the charge
Of carelessness — or worse, of ignorance.
Not every critic notices a spoiled line,
So anarchy's allowed our Roman poets.
Must I therefore write at random? Or suspect
That all can see the flaws, and play it safe
To stay in sight of pardon, dodging blame
But earning no praise? It is to Grecian models
You must return continually. You may boast
Your fathers praised the verse and wit of Plautus,
But they too readily admired both,
Too foolishly — while you and I know how
To tell an ugly from an elegant turn
Of phrase, to hear or scan a line correctly.
    They say that Thespis invented tragedy,
Til then unknown, and carted his poems about
In wagons for actors to perform, their faces
Smeared with wine lees. Aeschylus next devised
The mask, the stately robe, and raised a stage
On planks to teach them how tragedians strut.
Then followed Old Comedy, which won high praise,
But its freedoms slid into excess, to a violence
The law restrained. By law and to its shame
The chorus was silenced, forbidden to harm or insult.
    There's not a style our poets have left untried —
Even won fame when the Greek way was foregone
For the deeds of home, our high Roman drama
Or low Roman farce, the native themes and dress.
Our power would be felt no less in letters
Than in valor if our poets, one and all,
Didn't balk at the lag and labor of the file.

You must then, sons of Pompilius, reject
The poem that many days, many versions
Haven't refined, or pared down to the quick.
    Because Democritus believed that genius
Far surpasses mere art and banished the earnest
Sorts from Helicon, too many bards
Today don't cut their nails or clip their beards,
Don't bathe, prefer the corner table—as if,
By keeping their heads neither sane nor trimmed,
To win thereby the fabled name of poet.
Fool that I am, I purge my bile each spring.
Nothing else produces better poems.
But is it worth the cost? Better to play
The grindstone's part, useless for cutting but able
To sharpen steel. I may write nothing myself
But I shall teach the writer's trade and duties:
Where strength resides, what nourishes the poet,
What's proper, what's not, where truth and error lead.
    The source of all good writing still is knowledge.
Your subject's to be found in Socrates,
And the matter once in hand, the words will follow.
Having learned what's owed to friends and country,
What love is due a parent, a brother, a guest,
What the offices are of senator and judge,
Or of the general sent to war, a poet
Then can render each appropriately.
And yet the learned student has to take
Life itself as his book, and from it draw forth
A living language. Lacking charm or depth,
The play with vivid characters and strong
Scenes will hold and please the public better
Than all your chiming, precious, frothy verses.
    The Muse gave genius to the Greeks, the masters
Of eloquence and followers of fame.
Roman boys all learn the decimal system.
"Let young Albanus answer. If from five-twelfths

One be subtracted, what remains? Speak up."
"A third." "Good. You'll be able to account
For yourself. And if one is added, what results?"
"A half." And once this anxious greed infects
The soul, can we hope for poems to be written
Worth smoothing with cedar oil and storing in cypress?
     To instruct or delight must be the poet's aim,
Or to sound at once both pleasing and practical.
But when you teach, be terse: what's quickly said
The mind grasps readily and faithfully keeps;
A full mind overflows with excess words.
The fictions that satisfy are nearest the truth.
A story can't indulge its every fancy,
Can't pull a baby from Lamia's glutted belly.
Older readers scorn the frivolous,
The gentry don't want poems too severe—
That poet pleases all who mingles the useful
And graceful, who both advises and allures.
His book enriches dealers and crosses seas
To carry the author's fame to distant days.
     Certain faults exist we'd gladly pardon:
The string won't always yield the tone a hand
And mind intend, goes sharp instead of flat;
A bow may miss the target it's aiming for.
When most of a poem shines, I'm not offended
By smudges negligence has overlooked
Or plain ineptitude can't wipe away.
My point is this: we blame the scribe who copies
Incorrectly after he's been warned,
Or laugh at that cithern-player again and again
Plucking the same wrong note. So too the poet
Who blunders through becomes a Choerilus
Whose few good lines will prompt a sudden smile.
And drowsiness will steal upon works too long—
It saddens me that even Homer nods.
     Poems are like pictures: one enchants

If you're standing close; another, if further back.
This one haunts the shadows; that one prefers
To be viewed in the light, unafraid of a critic's
Scrutiny. This one pleased just once;
That one, though ten times seen, still pleases.

    You, sir, as eldest son, though wise yourself
And properly trained by your father, take what I say
To heart: in certain fields we may tolerate
The average. A mediocre lawyer, say,
Without a Messalla's golden tongue or the skill
Of an Aulus Cascellius, can still be helpful.
But neither gods nor men, not even booksellers,
Can long endure the mediocre poet.
As at a banquet a raucous orchestra,
A heavy perfume, or seeds in bitter honey
Offend because a dinner goes best without them,
So too a poem—created to give the spirit
Joy—falling short of the top, sinks to the bottom.
A clumsy man avoids the sporting fields,
And if inept with discus, ball, or hoop,
Leaves them alone—no jeering crowd for him.
Yet incompetence never stopped a poet. Why should it?
He's free, well-born—and better, well-connected
Among the nobility, perhaps even a moral man.

    But you, you wouldn't do or say anything
Unwise, would you? You're the sensible type.
Whatever you write, first read it to critical ears,
To Maecius, to your father, or even to me,
Then put it back in the drawer for nine long years.
You can always destroy what you haven't yet published.
Once out in the world, a word will never return.

    Orpheus, the messenger of the gods,
Frightened woodland savages from slaughter
And their brutal ways, and so it's said he tamed
The lion and wild tiger. So too the fable
That Amphion, who built the Theban walls,

Could enchant enormous stones by the sound of his lyre
And move them where he wished. The ancient wisdom
Separated the sacred and profane,
Private and public, forbade wedding a stranger,
Set marriage rules, erected cities, and carved
The laws on wood. The poets then were thought
Divine, all honor paid their work. And later
Lofty Homer and Tyrtaeus fired hearts
For war. Oracles were revealed in verse,
The path of life made known, the favor of kings
Sought in Pierian songs, and festivals
Founded to mark the end of hard labor. No need
To blush for the Muse's lyre, Apollo's song.

    The question asked is whether art or nature
Makes a praiseworthy poem. I fail to see
What good is either mere raw genius or study
Not veined with nature's riches: each the other's
Help requires, a single-minded purpose.
The racetrack runner who strives to finish first
Trained hard and long when young, sweated and froze,
Abstained from wine and women. The flutist featured
At the Pythian games once practiced in fear of his teacher.
But now it's enough to say: "I write a marvelous
Poem, better than anyone's, not to be topped.
Why admit I don't know what I never learned?"

    Like the crier who draws a crowd to auction,
So too that wealthy, moneylending poet
Bids his flatterers make a profit out of him.
If it's true he hosts those lavish society dinners,
Stands the hack some credit or rescues him
From irksome lawsuits, I wonder if that happy man
Any longer knows his true friends from his false.
If you've given or mean to give anyone anything,
Don't hand him your poems while he's pocketing it.
Of course he'll squeal: "Lovely! Bravo! Perfect!"
He'll go pale, tears in his sympathetic eyes,

Will jump or stamp his foot. As hired mourners
Wail at funerals more than those in grief,
So the mocker is moved more than the admirer.
Princes are said to force another cup
Of wine on those they want to prove are worthy
Of friendship. If you crow about your poems,
Beware the fox that always lurks below.

    Anything read to Quintilius would prompt
"Correct this, please. This too." If after a few
Attempts in vain, you confessed you couldn't do better,
He'd bid you scratch it out, at once return
Such ill-formed verses to the anvil. If still
You preferred to defend the faulty lines, he'd waste
Not a word more to keep you from admiring
Your own unrivaled work. An honest man
Will censure both the limp and the stilted line.
With a slash of his pen he'll cut the careless passage,
Trim the florid finery, shed light
On the obscure, expose the ambiguities,
Mark what must be changed, and prove himself
A very Aristarchus—and never say,
"Why should I insult a friend with trifles?"
It's minor trifles lead to major trouble,
Once the bad reviews and sneering start.

    Sensible men will flee and fear to touch
The frenzied poet, as if he were infectious—
Mangy, jaundiced, rabid, even possessed.
Only children tag along behind to tease him.
And if, out wandering, belching sublimities,
He falls into a well like the birdcatcher
Intent on his prey, and cries for help, who'll care?
If someone should appear and offer rope,
"Who knows?" I'll say. "Perhaps he did it all
On purpose, doesn't want to be saved," and tell
The tale of Empedocles, who, dying to be thought
A god, cooly leapt into fiery Etna.

Give the poets leave to kill themselves.
To save a man against his will is murder.
He's tried before, and rescue won't help make
A man of him, or calm his craving for
A memorable end. It's still unclear
Why he goes on writing. Perhaps he pissed
On his father's ashes or sinfully defiled
Some sacred spot? At any rate, he's mad,
And like a bear with strength enough to break
His cage's bars, he sends the listeners running
From his recitals, book lover or blockhead.
If he catches hold of one, he reads him to death.
The leech will not let go till gorged with blood.

NOTES

Plautus: Titus Maccius Plautus (d. 184 B.C.), the most popular playwright of his time
and a master of Latin dialogue and wordplay, domesticated the Greek New Comedy
for Rome. Caecilius Statius (d. 168 B.C.) succeeded Plautus as Rome's leading comic
dramatist and was praised for his ingenuity and emotional force. Varius Rufus is
most famous for having edited the *Aeneid* on Augustus's orders after Vergil's death,
but he was also an important dramatist and poet, and a friend of Maecenas and
Horace. Publius Vergilius Maro (70–19 B.C.) was Rome's greatest poet. Horace
praised both Varius and Vergil in one of his *Satires* (I.x.), and in another (I.v.) called
them "animae qualis neque candidiores / terra tulit, neque quis me sit devinctior
alter" (brighter souls earth never bore, nor any more dear to me). Marcus Porcius
Cato (234–149 B.C.) was known as "Censorius" because of his stern but just govern-
ing policies and his moral rectitude. His literary talent is evident in his published
speeches and letters, as well as in *De Agri Cultura*, his treatise on viniculture. His
Origines, a history in seven books, helped found a Latin prose style. Quintus Ennius
(239–169 B.C.), called "the father of Roman poetry" and revered by all literary
Romans, established with his *Annals* the Greek hexameter in Latin, and provided a
vivid panorama of Roman history.

Archilochus: Little is known about the life of this seventh-century elegiac poet from
Paros, but he is traditionally credited with the first use of iambics, in his satires.

comic sock and tragic buskin: Socks were the soft slippers worn by comic actors; buskins
were the high, thick-soled boots worn by tragic actors in the classic drama. The
footwear had come to stand in for the type of play being performed, as it does in Ben
Jonson's tribute to Shakespeare:

And though thou hadst small *Latine*, and lesse *Greeke*,
From thence to honour thee, I would not seeke
For names; but call forth thund'ring *Aeschilus*,
Euripides, and *Sophocles* to us,
Paccuvius, *Accius*, him of *Cordova* dead,
To life againe, to heare thy Buskin tread,
And shake a Stage: Or, when thy Sockes were on,
Leave thee alone, for the comparison
Of all, that insolent *Greece*, or haughtie *Rome*
Sent forth, or since did from their ashes come.

Thyestes: At a banquet Thyestes was served the flesh of his own children by his brother Atreus, in revenge for an earlier theft. During the meal, the sun reversed its course in horror. Chremes is a miser in comedies by Fundanius. Telephus, son of Heracles, was wounded by Achilles on the way to Troy; when the suppurating wound was later also cured by Achilles—an oracle having predicted the wounder would be the healer—Telephus guided the Greeks to Troy. Peleus, the father of Achilles, as a young man had accidentally killed his brother and been exiled for the deed.

the ancient cyclic poets: Alexandrian scholars after 300 B.C. used this term to describe those poets who continued "the Trojan cycle" with a series of six more epics that supplement the *Iliad* and *Odyssey*. Though admired by their contemporaries, these poems—or what we know of them from surviving fragments—only demonstrate Homer's superiority as both poet and narrator.

a scrawny goat: The disputed etymology of the word τραγῳδία, meaning "goat song," has given rise to theories from Aristotle on. Some thought it meant that tragic singers were dressed in goatskins; others that tragedies were performed during the ritual sacrifice of a goat. Horace seems to adopt the version that has tragedians competing for a goat as prize. It was sometimes thought that Thespis had first been awarded one.

Davus: Davus is a common slave's name, and a stock comic character, as are the others mentioned here. Pythias is the clever girl who cheats her rich old master, Simo. Silenus is eldest and leader of the satyrs, sotted and lustful but full of wisdom. He was entrusted with the education of Dionysius.

Accius: Lucius Accius (170–85 B.C.) was a Roman poet and dramatist.

Thespis: Tradition has it that Thespis was the first actor to have stepped forward, masked, from the chorus to speak a prologue and set speeches. Horace's description of Thespis's performances—with their wagons and wine lees—may be confusing the origins of early comedy with those of tragedy.

Democritus: Democritus (c. 460–c. 362 B.C.), who championed the Atomist doctrine of his teacher Leucippus, was nicknamed "Wisdom" by his contemporaries because of his encyclopedic learning, which included Oriental lore. Later ages called him "the laughing philosopher." He thought that a "Whirl" charged and reformed the mere particles of the material world.

Pompilius: The Pisos claimed descent from Numa Pompilius, the second king of Rome, just as Maecenas liked to trace his origin to the old Etruscan kings.

cedar oil and cypress: Poems were written onto papyrus rolls. The resinous secretion of the cedar or juniper tree was applied to the unwritten side in order to prevent decay and bookworms. Valuable rolls would be kept in cases made of cypress wood.

Lamia: Once a beautiful queen beloved by Zeus, she turned into a hag after own children were killed by Hera; in lonely revenge, she would carry off and devour the children of others. Originally a Libyan legend, the story was used by Greek nurses to scare their charges. Keats—who said he was following an account in Burton's *Anatomy of Melancholy*—made a gorgeous vampire of his lamia, a nymph transformed into a serpent "Striped like a zebra, freckled like a pard, / Eyed like a peacock, and all crimson barred."

Choerilus: A poet of Iasos in Caria and a camp follower of Alexander the Great, whose victories he extolled in epic poems, Choerilus is used here by Horace as the type of bad poet who occasionally writes a good line. He is mentioned in another epistle (II.i.), but less to mock the flattering verses than the foolishness of the king who paid so lavishly for them.

even Homer nods: A fine example in English of how a poet's phrase becomes proverbial—like, say, Horace's own *carpe diem* or *nil admirari* or *ut pictura poesis*. The Latin line reads literally "whenever good Homer drowses." Pope's original, of course—by now permanently misquoted—slyly denies what Horace proposes: "Those oft are *Stratagems* which *Errors* seem, / Nor is it *Homer Nods*, but *We* that *Dream*."

Messalla: Marcus Valerius Messalla Corvinus, a historian and famed courtroom orator, was probably an acquaintance of Horace from their days in Athens. His probity was famed and his eloquence was said by Tacitus to have been milder, sweeter, more elaborate than Cicero's. Messalla, who was consul in 31 B.C. and had commanded the center of Octavian's fleet at Actium, was later the patron of Tibullus and himself an author of panegyrics. Aulus Cascellius, a generation older, was a jurist of the late Republic, noted by Macrobius more for his wit than his learning.

Maecius: Spurius Maecius Tarpa, a drama critic appointed by Pompey to decide which plays might be performed, was head of the Board of Poets. In one satire (I.x.), Horace mentions competing for Maecius's judgment himself at the Temple of the Muses, where new poetry was read.

Tytaeus: Tytaeus was a lame schoolmaster and elegiac poet whose war songs—fragments of which survive—were said to have helped the Spartans who sang them on the march during their Second Messenian War, around 650 B.C.

Quintilius: Quintilius Varus, the famed critic from Cremona, was friend to Horace and Vergil. In one ode (I.18) Horace had bid him plant grapevines at Tibur; in another (I.24), he sang a "lugubres cantus" to mourn his death.

Aristarchus: This polymathic textual scholar and Homeric critic of legendary severity flourished at Alexandria about 180 B.C.

Empedocles: Philosopher and mystagogue of the fifth century B.C., Empedocles held that Love and Strife control the sphere of the four elements. How the story started that he threw himself into the crater at Mount Etna is not known. An episode Horace here treats satirically Matthew Arnold treated tragically in his famous 1852 dramatic poem, in which—according to Arnold's note on the poem—the protagonist "becomes the victim of depression and overtension of mind, to the utter deadness of joy, grandeur, spirit, and animated life, he desires to die; to be reunited with the universe, before by exaggerating his human side he has become utterly estranged from it." It seems to have been precisely such an attitude that Horace had in mind to scorn.